Medical Records Use and Abuse

Heidi Tranberg

Research Associate
Clinical and Biomedical Computing Unit
University of Cambridge

Jem Rashbass

Director of Clinical and Biomedical Computing
University of Cambridge
Director of the Eastern Cancer Registry
and Information Centre

RADCLIFFE MEDICAL PRESS
Oxford • San Francisco

Radcliffe Publishing Ltd
18 Marcham Road
Abingdon
Oxon OX14 1AA
United Kingdom

www.radcliffe-oxford.com
Electronic catalogue and worldwide online ordering.

British Library Cataloguing in Publication Data

A catalogue record for this book is available from the British Library.

ISBN 1 85775 604 5

Typeset by Advance Typesetting Ltd, Oxford
Printed and bound by TJ International Ltd, Padstow, Cornwall

Contents

Foreword

It is always a relief when the information you need to address a problem arrives just in time. So it is with the timely publication of this book. The UK government has embarked on one of the world's most challenging IT projects – The National Programme for Information Technology – which will transform the delivery of healthcare across the National Health Service. Through the programme, patients will have a life-long electronic health record accessible from healthcare centres across the country and ultimately their own homes. The days of lost patient notes, repeated laboratory tests and unknown medication should become a thing of the past.

With these changes will come significant opportunities and challenges for the way we handle medical records. We must ensure that the safeguards are in place to protect patient confidentiality and that when we need to use medical information for purposes not directly related to an individual's own medical care, such as health service planning, performance monitoring and research, it is undertaken in a transparent and appropriate way.

This book provides the background and practical guide for all those of us who face these challenges. Written by a lawyer and a clinical informatician, it provides the fusion between the legal issues and the practical clinical ones. There are clear explanations of the current legal framework of the Data Protection and Freedom of Information Acts and the effects of Section 60 of the Health and Social Care Bill. These are set in the context of real-world applications; for example, there is guidance for those who need to develop consent forms for research or respond to requests from the public for healthcare information and there is extensive coverage of the rights of the patient who wishes to access their own records.

Several of the more complex issues that have a significant impact on policy are also dealt with in depth. A chapter is devoted to the complexities of anonymising data, how this might be implemented, the benefits that can be achieved and challenges arising from pseudonymisation. There is information for those involved in medical research and what they must do to guarantee that patients' rights are protected when they request or use clinical information. The background to 'consent' and the impact that implied and explicit consent can have on the way records are collected and used is particularly well covered.

This book has many audiences, all of whom will gain from the easily accessible information within it. Caldicott guardians, research ethics committee members, and all those researchers and clinicians who need to analyse patient information will have a particular need for this handbook. Patients and the public should use it to understand how their healthcare information is protected and used. Its arrival could not have come at a better time.

Sir John Pattison
Former Director of Research, Analysis and Information
Department of Health
March 2004

About the authors

Heidi Tranberg trained in both law and psychology, and worked for a number of years as a solicitor in a leading Australian law firm, specialising in intellectual property, information technology, biotechnology and privacy. During this time she played a key role in developing the firm's health privacy website. Since joining the Clinical and Biomedical Computer Unit at Cambridge University, Heidi has been involved in a variety of projects, including research of health privacy issues, strategic planning and marketing activities, and the development of an electronic dyslexia-screening test. She has published several papers and articles on legal and ethical issues.

Dr Jem Rashbass has a background in medicine, molecular biology and pathology. Since 1997 he has been Director of the Clinical and Biomedical Computing Unit at Cambridge University, a group responsible for developing novel computer applications in clinical teaching, practice and medical research. He is also the Director of the Eastern Cancer Intelligence Centre – providing cancer registration and analysis across the east of England, he holds an honorary consultant contract in histopathology at Addenbrooke's NHS Trust and is a Non-executive Director of the NHS Information Authority.

Acknowledgements

The authors greatly appreciate the assistance of a number of experts who generously shared their views and experiences on various issues discussed in the book. In particular, they would like to thank Professor Don Detmer and Baroness Onora O'Neill, both of the University of Cambridge; Marlene Winfield, Head of Patient and Citizen Relations at the NHS Information Authority; and Janine Brooks, a Caldicott Guardian at the NHS Information Authority.

Chapter 1

Introduction

Protecting the privacy of patient information is a major challenge facing the health sector. Today's patients expect, and are entitled by law to receive, a high standard of medical privacy. Given the complexity and function of the health system, however, it can be difficult to meet this expectation.

Healthcare is an information-rich activity, in that it involves the collection, use and disclosure of large quantities of sensitive personal data. Such information is not only required by health professionals directly involved in patient treatment, but also the many groups who indirectly contribute to the delivery of quality healthcare. Administrators, policy makers, researchers, educators, public health bodies and auditors are just some of the groups that require access to patient data to ensure that high quality, cost-effective medical treatment is delivered in a timely and appropriate manner. Making this information available, without compromising patients' rights, is a complex task.

How have health privacy rights evolved?

The right to personal privacy is not a new concept. It has been recognised for many years, and was even included in the 1948 United Nations Universal Declaration of Human Rights.[1] Initially, however, the right to privacy was more concerned with protecting people from unwanted intrusions into their personal lives, rather than inappropriate disclosures of their personal data.

As information came to play a larger role in society, this focus began to shift. The increased use of computers in the 1970s and 1980s brought new opportunities to store and analyse large volumes of data, and prompted interest in individuals' right to control the use and dissemination of their personal information, a right often referred to as 'informational privacy'.[2] In light of the circumstances that caused this type of privacy to be recognised, in the UK protection was originally limited to data that were stored electronically.* As many medical records still were stored in paper files, this development had only a limited effect on patient data privacy.

In many countries, various disease- or condition-specific privacy acts also provided some assurance of privacy,** although these acts had only a fairly limited impact on the overall level of protection of patient data. This was partly because the special protection was only extended to information relating to a limited number of conditions, usually those considered particularly sensitive or potentially damaging to a patient's reputation, such as mental illness or sexually transmitted disease. In many cases, protecting patients' privacy was also not the sole, or even major, concern of these disease-specific acts, with mandatory reporting obligations often being imposed in addition to restrictions on disclosure.† The protection provided by disease-specific privacy legislation, therefore, was limited and piecemeal, and did little to recognise patients' rights to informational privacy.

For many medical records the greatest source of privacy protection continued to be doctors' general duty of confidentiality. This duty prevents doctors from using or disclosing confidential information obtained within the confines of the doctor–patient relationship for any purpose other than that for which it was provided. In theory, the duty of confidentiality should prevent medical information obtained for the purpose of treating a patient from being used for any secondary purpose without the patient's permission. In practice, however, it did not always provide such a comprehensive level of protection. This was caused in part by a tendency to interpret the obligation in accordance with the paternalistic approach to medicine that prevailed at the time, which often resulted in patients' rights or wishes taking second place to doctors' professional judgement.[3] It was standard practice in most institutions to use medical records for a range of secondary purposes, such as audit, research and administrative activities, without consent – either on the assumption that consent was not required (as the use posed little risk to patients) or that it could be implied from patients' actions. In any event, it was often very difficult for patients to monitor the way in which their medical records were used, as they did not usually have a right to verify

---

* The Data Protection Act 1984 Section 1 defines 'data' as 'information recorded in a form in which it can be processed by equipment operating automatically in response to instructions given for that purpose'.

** For example, in the UK, identifying information about a patient who is being treated for venereal disease may not be disclosed other than to a medical practitioner in connection with the patient's treatment or to prevent the spread of the disease (NHS (Venereal Disease) Regulations 1974 and NHS Trusts (Venereal Diseases) Directions 1991).

† In the UK, for example, there is a mandatory requirement for any practitioner who performs an abortion to notify the Chief Medical Officer. The same legislation then goes on to restrict the extent to which the information contained in such a notice can be disclosed. (Abortion Act 1967 Section 2 and Abortion Regulations 1991 Sections 4 and 5.)

what had been recorded about them or how it had been disclosed; often, there was not even a record of the disclosures that had been made.*

This situation has changed substantially in the last decade. Information privacy is now recognised to a greater extent than ever before – a development principally led by international initiatives. Following the adoption of data protection agreements by the Council of Europe[4] and the Organisation for Economic Co-operation and Development (OECD)[5] in the 1980s, in 1995 the European Community developed a new binding Directive setting out a number of data protection principles.[6] The Directive required signatory countries to establish national legislation implementing its terms. In the UK, this was achieved by the enactment of the Data Protection Act 1998, which came into effect on 1 March 2000. As the Directive imposed restrictions on the transfer of personal data to countries that did not have equivalent data protection regimes, it also prompted change outside the EU.

Today, most European and other industrialised countries have established, or are moving toward, comprehensive data protection legislation.[7] Although there are a number of differences, both minor and significant, between the specific legislation adopted in each country, the general approach tends to be quite similar. Most countries have established a single regime for protecting all types of personal data, whether financial, educational, social or otherwise, with only minor concessions given to the greater sensitivity of some types of data, such as that pertaining to health. The exception to this trend is the US, where medical information is protected by specific federal legislation.**

Since the 1995 EC Directive, further international agreements governing the privacy of health information have been signed.[†] In the UK, however, the most significant restriction on the way information is collected and managed continues to be the Data Protection Act 1998 and the various policies and guidelines that seek to implement its terms.

---

*This is because medical records are usually considered to be the property of the health provider, not the patient. Under the common law, doctors are only required to grant patients access to their medical record if doing so is necessary to fulfil the doctor's duty to act in the patient's best interest (R v Mid Glamorgan Family Health Services Authority (1995) 1 All ER 356).

** Health Insurance Portability and Accountability Act 1996. However, this legislation only applies to a limited number of entities that could potentially control health information, namely health plans, healthcare providers that electronically transmit healthcare information, and healthcare clearing houses. For information controlled by other types of organisations, the level of protection will depend upon the applicable state law.

† Under the 1997 Council of Europe's Convention on Human Rights and Biomedicine, for example, a new right 'not to be informed about health information' was included in the concept of 'respect for private life and the right to information'.

What information is recorded about patients?

Medical records are an important and comprehensive source of information about all aspects of an individual's health. Traditionally, however, particularly in primary care, medical records were relatively brief documents, used mainly to refresh the doctor's memory.[8] Very detailed information was not required as doctors tended to be well-acquainted with patients and their families, often knowing more about their patients' medical histories than the patients themselves. In recent years, however, the nature of medical records has changed substantially.

First, there has been a significant increase in the amount and type of information included in medical records. Advances in medical knowledge and diagnostic techniques have enabled doctors to uncover much more information about individuals' health status, all of which must be documented. In some cases, these developments have made it possible for entirely new types of information, such as genetic data, to be collected. It has also become common practice for doctors to record more non-medical information about patients, such as lifestyle choices and family history, in response to the increasing evidence of the effects of such factors on health.

There has also been a change in the manner in which information is recorded, with greater emphasis being placed on more complete, detailed and consistent documentation. This largely is attributable to the increase in the number of people involved in the care of patients, both over their lifetime and during a single care episode, which has arisen from the increased specialisation of the medical profession, the delivery of care through medical teams, and the greater mobility of society.[9] (Estimates in the US suggest that 150 people will look at a patient's medical record during a stay in hospital.)[10] As a result, the primary role of medical records is no longer that of a memory aid, but a vital communication tool, needed to share detailed and varied information amongst a potentially wide range of health professionals. In addition, the increased risk of legal challenge brought about by the growing number of medical negligence claims has prompted doctors to document their findings and decisions more fully. For example, it is now standard practice for significant, negative, clinical results to be recorded explicitly, rather than to assume that they are negative by omission.

In addition to these changes there has also been an increase in the use of medical records for secondary purposes not directly connected with the provision of care.[9] Doctors are now only one of the many groups of people with legitimate interests in accessing this important source of data. Identifiable patient information is used routinely for the purpose of clinical and financial audits, health service planning, resource management, authenticating health providers' payment claims and patients' health insurance claims, rehabilitation and social welfare programmes, and education and training. Information from medical records is also used extensively in epidemiological and health service research, and for the purpose of disease monitoring. With the rise in personal injury, child custody and other types of litigation, it has also become increasingly common for medical records to be accessed via compulsory court processes.[11] Added to this is the growing number of new users of health information, such as medical and surgical suppliers and pharmaceutical and information technology companies.[8]

Although the protection of medical records may not be a new issue, therefore, changes in the health industry have altered its nature and importance.

Why protect the privacy of health information?

The primary reason for respecting the privacy of health information is to protect patients from the negative effects brought about by the loss of personal privacy. Medical records contain intimate and sensitive information, which, if inappropriately used or shared, could embarrass or distress patients, and even cause them financial or other damage (*see* p. 23). Fearing the unwanted exposure of personal information, patients may also avoid medical treatment or withhold facts from their doctor, both of which could have serious health consequences.[12]

In many cases, however, using or disclosing medical information poses little, if any, risk to patients. Providing that basic security procedures are followed, such as anonymising identifiable data and storing data securely, the use of patients' information for research, audit or planning purposes is unlikely to cause them damage or distress, and may even provide some indirect benefit.[13] This does not mean that providing this protection ceases to be important, as there are still persuasive moral and ethical arguments for respecting informational privacy.

It is claimed, for example, that there is a strong connection between protecting the privacy of personal information, and the concept of personal autonomy.[9,12,14] Protecting privacy tends to increase individuals' confidence in their ability to control and manage the direction of their lives, a development that sits well with the modern view of healthcare as being centred on the rights of the patient. Many patients place a high value on the privacy of their personal information, in particular that relating to health, with the right to control how it is used often considered as fundamental as the right to make decisions about their private behaviour. Giving patients control over their personal information demonstrates an understanding and respect for their status as an autonomous and free-thinking patient, which is likely to increase their satisfaction with the health system and their belief in its ability to provide a high quality service.

These arguments capture the emotional and human components of privacy and explain the importance of ensuring it is protected, but they do not address the more difficult issue of how this protection should be achieved.

How should health information be protected?

Numerous studies, reports and debates have investigated the best way of protecting patient information. From these, several basic principles have emerged. It is generally accepted, for example, that patients should be kept informed of, and given some control over, the way in which their information is used, and that data should only be disclosed on a 'need to know' basis.[15] Attempts to formulate the specific policies and rules needed to implement these principles, however, have revealed a significant divergence in views. Devising general principles (it seems) is much easier than agreeing on specific requirements.

This problem is well illustrated by the diversity of opinion concerning the circumstances in which individuals' rights to privacy should be overridden. Most people, be they patients, healthcare providers or policy makers, agree that there must be some limits on individuals' right to control the way their information is used. To maintain a safe and functional society, and to protect the well-being of those living within it, it is essential that certain groups are given access to some types of information, irrespective of patients' wishes. Apprehending and prosecuting criminals, providing emergency medical treatment and maintaining population disease registers are just three vital activities that would be jeopardised if access to information was always dependent upon individuals' agreement.

Accepting that there should be exceptions to the requirements of the Data Protection Act 1998, however, is not the same as agreeing upon the nature of those exceptions. Does the possibility of a medical breakthrough, for example, justify research being carried out on patient data without patients' permission? Would the situation be different depending upon the importance of the condition being investigated and the researcher's confidence of finding a cure? Equally, does the need to prevent and detect crimes justify the disclosure of patients' information in all circumstances, or only in relation to particularly serious offences, in which case, how is 'seriousness' measured? No matter how necessary or important an exception may be, determining its exact nature and scope will always be a matter of some contention.

Differences of opinion have also arisen in relation to the programmes and policies needed to deal with other aspects of medical record privacy. There is much uncertainty, for example, as to the best way to inform patients of the way in which their information is used and to obtain their consent for this (*see* Chapter 3). There is also disagreement over the level of anonymity of data that is needed to protect patients' identities, and the control, if any, that patients should have over this type of information (*see* Chapter 10).

Much of the difficulty in obtaining consensus arises from the large number and variety of people who will be affected by the rules and policies that are ultimately implemented. Nearly everyone is involved in the health system as a patient, a professional, or both, and their experiences vary considerably. The different views of clinicians, researchers, medical bodies, privacy advocates and patient groups reflect their different interests in accessing (or preventing access to) information, and the way in which increased privacy will assist or hamper their aims. Even patients with different healthcare experiences have divergent views.[16] More often than not, groups that seek extended rights to access personal information, such as administrators and researchers, do so for very worthy purposes, whereas those advocating increased privacy protection also have valid reasons or concerns.

To ensure that the rules can apply widely, the privacy requirements in many healthcare directives and guidelines have been drafted in fairly general terms. For example, the government's new plan for information-sharing in the public services promises to give citizens a choice over how their personal information is used, 'wherever possible'.[17] Although this avoids controversy in the short term, and gives the government considerable flexibility when implementing the rules in the future, it does little to clarify the rules that will apply. Whether this provides an acceptable level of privacy protection depends entirely upon the government's interpretation of what is 'possible'.

The Data Protection Act 1998

The Data Protection Act 1998 regulates the collection, use and disclosure of information that relates to identifiable individuals (called 'personal data'). It does this by establishing eight privacy rules – known as the 'data protection principles' – with which anyone controlling personal data (called 'data controllers') must comply. Among other things, these principles provide that information must only be collected and used fairly, lawfully and for one of the purposes, or in compliance with one of the conditions, set out in the Act.* In practice, this often means that data controllers have to obtain individuals' consent if they wish to collect or use any data about them.

Data controllers are also required to give individuals basic information, at the time of collection, about who will use the data and the purpose or purposes for which it will be used.** They cannot subsequently use that data in any manner incompatible with those purposes (the second data protection principle). The Act also imposes restrictions on the amount of information collected (the third data protection principle) and the manner in which it is stored (the seventh data protection principle), and grants individuals certain rights in respect of their information, including the right to verify what has been recorded about them and how it has been used.[†] The data protection principles are considered in further detail in Box 1.1 and a flowchart summarising the main decisions to be made before using potentially personal data is provided in Figure 1.1 (*see* page 10).

Box 1.1

Data Protection Act 1998: glossary and the data protection principles

The Data Protection Act 1998 requires all data controllers to comply with the data protection principles when processing personal data. Key terms used in the Act include:

- *Data* – information recorded or stored, either electronically or in a relevant filing system (a set of information about individuals that is structured so that information about a particular individual is readily accessible). This definition would cover much of the information held by healthcare providers, including medical records, appointment books and staff files.
- *Personal data* – data from which a living person can be identified. This covers both data that identify a person (such as a medical record containing a patient's name), as well as data that identify a person when read in conjunction with other information which is likely to be available to the person accessing it. The NHS Number is classified as personal data, therefore, despite the fact that it does not reveal a patient's identity, as the information needed to identify the patient can be obtained relatively easily through the NHS Tracing Service.

---

* First data protection principle. The purposes and conditions are listed in the Data Protection Act 1998, Sections 2 and 3.
** Data Protection Act 1998, paragraphs 2 and 3, Schedule 1, Part 2.
[†] Data Protection Act 1998, Section 7.

- *Data controller* – the person or organisation that determines the purpose for which, or manner in which, personal data will be processed. There may be more than one data controller for a single item of personal data.
- *Data subject* – the individual who is the subject of the personal data. A data subject must be a living person, but need not be a UK citizen.
- *Processing* – collecting, recording, holding, altering, using, disclosing, transmitting, erasing or destroying data.

In a simplified form, the data protection principles require that personal data:

1 are processed fairly and lawfully
2 are only processed for one or more specified and lawful purposes; data cannot be used or disclosed for any purpose incompatible with the specified purposes for which it was collected, without the permission of the data subject
3 are adequate, relevant and not excessive for the purpose for which they are required
4 are accurate and up to date
5 are not kept any longer than is necessary for the purpose for which they are required
6 are processed in accordance with the rights of the data subject under the Data Protection Act 1998. These include: the right to access any personal data held about them; to prevent processing of data that is likely to cause them damage or distress; and to prevent processing for the purpose of direct marketing
7 are protected from unauthorised or unlawful processing or loss
8 are not transferred to countries outside the European Union that do not have adequate data protection laws.

For healthcare providers, the first and second of these principles will usually be the most important. These are discussed in greater detail in Chapter 3, *see* Box 3.1.

The Data Protection Act gives some concession to the private and intimate nature of health information by including it in a special class of personal data, known as sensitive data, to which more stringent conditions apply.* When collecting sensitive data, for example, data controllers must, in addition to the usual obligations, satisfy one of a number of extra conditions

---

*Data Protection Act 1998, Section 2.

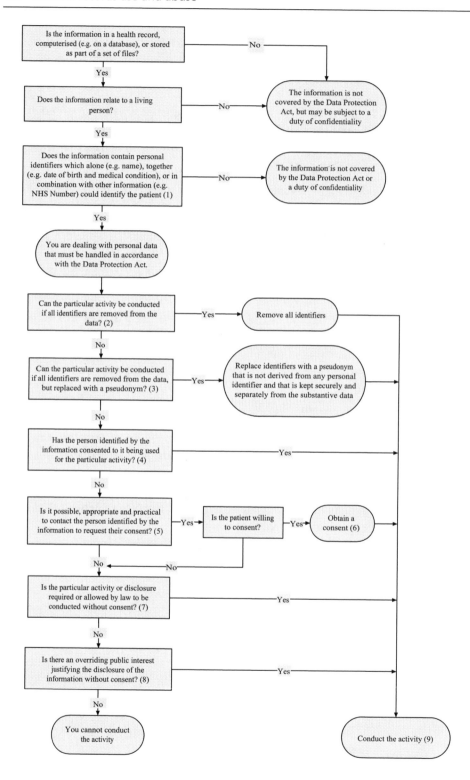

set out in the Act.* For the most part, however, the same privacy regime applies to all types of personal data.

The Data Protection Act has been criticised on a number of grounds.[18] Many commentators argue that it is inappropriate for dealing with the particular considerations relevant to health information, it having been written principally for the financial and commercial sectors. Relying on consent as the main means of controlling the use that can be made of personal information, it is suggested, is not the optimum method for addressing privacy concerns in the health sector, as patients often lack the knowledge, experience, understanding or confidence to determine how their health information should be used.[19] A number of the requirements of the Act are also quite uncertain or ambiguous, making it difficult for healthcare providers and those advising them to implement appropriate privacy policies.[20] For example, while it is clear that anonymous data are not covered by the data protection requirements, the Data Protection Act 1998 does not clarify

---

Figure 1.1 (opposite): The 1998 Data Protection Act. The flowchart summarises the main decisions that need to be made before using or disclosing information. The issues are presented in a simplified form to provide a general overview of the topic. The flowchart is not intended to provide a full summary of, or a comprehensive guide to, the Data Protection Act. Key: 1 = *see* Chapter 10, in particular p. 132; 2 = the Caldicott Committee definition of an identifier, *see* Chapter 10, p. 131. Examples include names, addresses, telephone numbers, email addresses, date of birth, NHS numbers, local hospital codes, bank account details and employers' or family members' names or contact details; 3 = *see* Chapter 10, pp 132–4; 4 = *see* Chapter 3, p. 32. Consent can be express or implied, although for some activities or disclosures (such as those that are likely to be controversial or to affect patients directly) it may be better to obtain express consent (*see* Chapter 3, p. 33 and pp 36–8). The activity must also be covered by the scope of the consent (*see* Chapter 3, p. 34); 5 = relevant considerations include: the cost, time and effort required to contact each patient (affected by the numbers of patients and the age and currency of the records); the likelihood that contacting the patients wil be distressing for patients and their families; the likelihood that a significant number of patients may have died; 6 = *see* 4 above; 7 = legislation that may allow or require the disclosure of identifiable health information includes the Abortion Act 1967, the Terrorism Act 2000 and the regulations made under the Health and Social Care Act 2001 (Section 60), *see* Chapter 7, pp 95–6 and Chapter 8, pp 110–11. The disclosure of patient information may also be required under the terms of a witness summons or other court order (*see* Chapter 9, p. 117); 8 = *see* Chapter 8; 9 = it will be necessary to comply with additional requirements set out in other legislation or other relevant ethical guidelines. For example, in the case of research, ethics review board approval will be required.

---

* The additional conditions are contained in the Data Protection Act 1998, Schedule 3.

what standard of anonymity needs to be met. Despite relying quite heavily on the concept of individual consent, it also fails to give any guidance about the type of consent required and how specific it should be.

Added to these concerns is the continuing controversy over the many exceptions and exemptions that enable data controllers and government bodies to avoid the data protection requirements. Although most of the exceptions actually contained in the Act only arise in relatively specific circumstances, more recent legislation has given the government additional powers to avoid the requirements of the Act.* Many people fear that despite the government's assurances to the contrary, this power will be used too extensively (*see* Chapter 7, p. 96).

In the healthcare sector, problems with compliance further challenge the effectiveness of the Data Protection Act 1998. Despite the Act having been in force for a number of years, the National Health Service (NHS) is yet to modify its practices to comply fully with the new requirements. According to the Information Commissioner, who oversees the administration of the Act, the NHS frequently breaches the legislation by using identifiable patient information without patients' knowledge or consent.[15] This practice, it is suggested, results from an overriding belief within the NHS that the sharing of information benefits many, harms few and is essential for efficiency and expediency.[15] This belief is reinforced by the low regard given to information management within the NHS, as well as a lack of informatics training in the health sector generally. The effect of this is a poor understanding of, and commitment to, the management of patient information.[21]

There is also some uncertainty under the Data Protection Act 1998 with regard to the ownership of personal data. Although the issue of data ownership is relatively straightforward where medical records are created and stored locally, the idea of a national electronic health record, which is part of the government's current proposals, makes this much more complex. If information is collected and entered into the system by patients' general practitioners, but is then stored at the primary care trust level, who is the relevant owner? Does ownership change as data are collated, aggregated and analysed? The Data Protection Act avoids this issue by imposing obligations on 'data controllers', being those who can determine the purpose and manner in which data are used, rather than 'data owners'. However, as a single piece of information can be controlled by a number of different data controllers, there is likely to be much confusion and conflict about privacy and data management responsibilities.

These problems show that, although the Data Protection Act is a key consideration in the issue of medical record privacy, it does not, on its own,

---

* Health and Social Care Act 2001, Section 60.

provide a complete solution to the existing confusion and disagreement. Of equal importance is the way in which the courts and ethical bodies interpret the Act, the specific policies and plans that are developed to deal with the data protection requirements, and the extent to which these are implemented and enforced. A key component of this is the government's proposed changes to the NHS.

The government's proposal

As part of the government's plan to modernise the NHS, it has developed a new strategy, known as 'Information for Health', which deals with data protection and other information management issues within the NHS.[21, 22] The strategy, which runs from 1998 until 2005, aims to redesign the NHS around the patient.

Under the new plan, information is recognised as a vital factor in the delivery of healthcare, with the ability to provide quality patient care said to be dependent on 'the availability of good information, accessible when and where it is needed'. Without this, a health system is said to be 'at best inefficient and frustrating and at worst dangerous'.[23] The plan therefore aims to improve the way the NHS uses data, and increase data-sharing both within the NHS and with other government organisations.

At the same time, the government also recognises the sensitivity of the information involved in healthcare. It therefore plans to achieve this increased data-sharing in a way that ensures privacy is enhanced, not derogated. Individual deliverables, such as introducing life-long electronic health records, establishing 24-hour online access to patients' records and providing seamless care through the sharing of information between general practitioners, hospitals and community care providers, must all be met without damaging patients' privacy expectations. It remains to be seen whether this will be achieved.

Summary

- Interest in protecting the privacy of personal data, including health data, has increased in recent years.
- More information is collected about patients today than ever before.
- There is relatively high agreement on the general principles that should govern the protection of medical data, but it is much harder to agree on the specific rules and policies.
- The Data Protection Act 1998 is a key consideration but does not provide a complete solution to the problem of medical record privacy.

References

1 United Nations (1948) *Universal Declaration of Human Rights*, Article 12. Adopted and proclaimed by General Assembly resolution no. 217 A (III), 10 December.

2 Health Privacy Working Group (1999) *Best Principles for Health Privacy*. Institute for Health Care Research and Policy, Health Privacy Project, Georgetown University. (www.healthprivacy.org/usr_doc/33807.pdf). (Accessed 24 August 2003.)

3 Coulter A (1999) Paternalism or partnership. *British Medical Journal*. **319**: 719.

4 Council of Europe (1981) Convention for the Protection of Individuals with Regard to the Automatic Processing of Data.

5 Organisation for Economic Co-operation and Development (OECD) (1980) *Guidelines on the Protection of Privacy and Transborder Data Flows of Personal Data*. OECD, France.

6 EC Directive 95/46/EC (1995) On the protection of individuals with regard to the processing of personal data and on the free movement of such data. 24 October.

7 Cushman F and Detmer D (1998) Information policy for the US health sector: engineering, political economy and ethics. *Milbank Quarterly Special Edition Electronic Article*, January. (www.milbank.org/art). (Accessed 5 September 2003.)

8 Committee on Maintaining Privacy and Security in Healthcare Applications of the National Information Infrastructure, National Research Council (1997) *For the Record: protecting electronic health information*. National Academy Press, Washington DC.

9 Institute of Medicine (1994) *Health Data in the Information Age*. National Academy Press, Washington DC.

10 George S (2002) Medical privacy and medical research. *CLA-GAB Newsletter of the Cancer and Leukaemia Group B.* **11**: 2.

11 Lowrence W (1997) *Privacy and Health Research (A Report to the US Secretary of Health and Human Services),* May. (http://aspe.hhs.gov/datacncl/PHR.htm). (Accessed 16 June 2003.)

12 Wynia M, Coughlin S, Alpert S *et al.* (2001) Shared expectations for the protection of identifiable health care information. *Journal of General Internal Medicine.* **16**: 100.

13 Lawlor D and Stone T (2001) Public health and data protection: an inevitable collision or potential for a meeting of minds? *International Journal of Epidemiology.* **30**: 1221.

14 Institute of Medicine (2000) *Protecting Data Privacy in Health Services Research.* National Academy Press, Washington DC.

15 Department of Health (DoH) (2001) *Building the Information Core: protecting and using confidential patient information – a strategy for the NHS.* (www.doh.gov.uk/ipu/confiden/strategyv7.pdf). (Accessed 10 June 2003.)

16 NHS Information Authority, The Consumers' Association, Health Which? (2002) *Share with Care – people's views on consent and confidentiality of patient information.* (www.nhsia.nhs.uk/confidentiality/pages/docs/swc.pdf). (Accessed 20 August 2003.)

17 Performance and Innovation Unit (2002) *Privacy and Data Sharing: the way forward for public services.* April: 5. (www.number-10.gov.uk/su/privacy/index.htm). (Accessed 10 April 2003.)

18 Knoppers B (2000) Appendix D – Confidentiality of health information: international comparative approaches. In: Institute of Medicine, *Protecting Data Privacy in Health Services Research.* National Academy Press, Washington DC.

19 Starr P (1999) Privacy and access to information: striking the right balance in healthcare. In: *Massachusetts Health Data Consortium, 4th Annual Meeting,* Boston, MA, 16 April. (www.nchica.org/HIPAAResources/Samples/privacylessons/P-101%20Massachusetts%20Health%20Data%20Consortium.htm). (Accessed 13 September 2003.)

20 Strobl J, Cave E and Walley T (2000) Data protection legislation: interpretation and barriers to research. *British Medical Journal.* **321**: 890.

21 NHS Information Authority (1998) *Information for Health.* (www.nhsia.nhs.uk/def/pages/info4health/contents.asp). (Accessed 10 June 2003.)

22 Department of Health (DoH) (2001) *Building the Information Core: implementing The NHS Plan.* (www.doh.gov.uk/ipu/strategy/overview/overview.pdf). (Accessed 10 June 2003.)

23 NHS Information Authority (2002) *Caring for Information – model for the future,* para 1.3. (www.nhsia.nhs.uk/confidentiality/pages/consultation/docs/caring_model.pdf). (Accessed 8 July 2003.)

Chapter 2

Is there a medical privacy crisis?

The importance of protecting the privacy of medical information is not a new concept; it has been recognised since the time of Hippocrates. Recently, however, public concern about this subject appears to have grown, with medical privacy emerging as an important political and social issue. In part, this is attributable to the dramatic increase in the capacity of computers to store and share information, as well as the advances in medical knowledge that have increased the amount, diversity and intimacy of information collected for healthcare, and what that information can reveal. There has also been an increase in the number of people and organisations involved in providing care to a single individual, resulting in a significant amount of legitimate data-sharing. In the modern world it is almost impossible to calculate the amount of information held about an individual, let alone determine how it is used and secured.

Threats to privacy

The confidentiality of medical records is threatened in many different ways. Most newsworthy is the misappropriation and disclosure of medical records for financial gain or to cause harm or embarrassment. Contrary to popular belief, these types of disclosures are usually carried out with the co-operation of someone who is authorised to access the necessary information, rather than through the surreptitious activity of computer hackers. Although these types of disclosures are relatively uncommon, they have the potential to cause significant harm to the patients affected, and can generate substantial media exposure, which damages the public's trust in health data security.

Much more prevalent, and arguably a greater threat to privacy, is healthcare providers using or disclosing medical data, without patients' consent, for additional purposes unrelated to patients' care and treatment (commonly called 'secondary purposes'). Patient information is routinely disclosed to organisations not directly involved in patients' care, such as health service researchers, public health agencies and, in some countries, insurers.

In most cases, the use of patients' information for these types of activities is not in itself objectionable, as the purposes being pursued are often commendable and will not normally cause patients any physical or financial harm. In fact, they may even provide some indirect benefit. Not surprisingly, if asked, many patients would be happy for their records to be used for secondary purposes. Problems arise, however, because patients are not always given this option. Healthcare providers often fail to be fully open with patients about how their medical records will be used, meaning that many secondary uses of information occur without patients' knowledge or consent. This is likely to damage public trust in the security and confidentiality of health data, and to create an atmosphere of suspicion. According to a 1997 US report,[1] it is this type of disclosure that poses the most significant threat to the confidentiality of patient information.

There have also been reports, mostly within the USA, of healthcare data being used for wholly inappropriate secondary purposes. For example, according to a US survey, 35% of Fortune 500 companies have considered health records in making employment-related decisions.[2] Although inappropriate uses of this kind are less common than other types of secondary uses, they are much more likely to cause patients significant harm.

The final threat to the privacy of healthcare data comes from the inadvertent release of patient information through poor hospital procedures or practices. Gossiping, discussing patients in open areas, leaving records lying around or displayed on computer screens and failing to collect faxes immediately can all lead to the spread of sensitive, identifiable data. Although no malice is intended, these activities could cause patients significant damage or distress.

Examples of breaches of privacy are given in Box 2.1.

Box 2.1

Examples of privacy breaches

- A secondhand laptop memory stick, purchased by a UK estate agent, was found to contain the confidential clinical records for 13 cancer patients treated at the Royal Bolton Hospital in Greater Manchester. The records included patients' names, addresses, dates of birth, gender and, in some cases, NHS numbers and family histories of cancer. The Bolton Royal Hospitals NHS Trust apologised for the breach of confidentiality, but claimed it did not use memory devices of that kind.[3]

- The 13-year-old daughter of a US hospital employee took a list of patients' names and phone numbers from the hospital when visiting her mother. As a joke, she contacted the patients to tell them they were HIV positive.[4]
- A new IT system installed in a UK hospital mistakenly allowed general access to all laboratory tests ordered by general practitioners. As a result, sensitive information, such as HIV test results, was available to a wide range of hospital employees. The error was discovered when a nurse found her own test results on the system.[5]
- In Australia, a customer services officer for the government health plan, Medicare, was accused of accessing the personal details and Medicare histories of up to 90 people a day. During legal proceedings in 2001, he explained his behaviour on the basis that he had been bored.[5]
- Several thousand identifiable patient records at the University of Michigan Medical Center were accidentally posted on public internet sites. Despite the Center's security protocols, it did not become aware of the error until notified by journalists two months later.[6]
- A banker who served on his county's health board in the USA cross-referenced customer accounts with patient information and called due mortgages of any customers suffering from cancer.[7]
- In 2002, an Australian health insurance company sent letters to a large number of Australian employers, mistakenly containing a form detailing a named member's serious medical condition, rather than a sample form with non-specific information.[8]

Society's attitude

Findings within the UK and abroad indicate an overall rise in the number of people concerned about privacy.[9] In a survey by the UK Information Commissioner, 96% of respondents rated privacy as very or quite important, with 73% concerned about the amount of information recorded about them.[10] Although compared with other issues, data protection is not a topic that provokes strong spontaneous feelings, it does emerge as an area of concern if people are prompted.[10] When presented with a list of issues, only crime and education standards are considered to be more important.

Despite these findings, most people in the UK are confident in the extent to which the confidentiality of healthcare data is protected.[11] Most patients place significant trust in doctors, and understand and accept the need for information to be shared within the NHS. Concerns rise, however, when information is transferred outside the NHS, such as when work is contracted out to a third party. Not surprisingly, opinions about healthcare privacy differ considerably according to patients' age, education level, health status and familiarity with technology.* Attitudes are also influenced by the type of healthcare information in question, with greater importance placed on the need to protect particularly sensitive data, such as genetic information.[12]

A similar rise in public concerns about privacy has been found in the USA. According to American research, most people believe that it is harder today than in the past to keep personal information such as medical details confidential. The level of protection they believe is afforded to their privacy varies significantly depending upon the type of organisation holding it. Although most people trust doctors, hospitals and other health professionals to keep personal information confidential all or most of the time, there is a reasonably high level of distrust when it comes to private health plans and government programmes such as Medicare.[13] In addition, 20% of American adults believe that a healthcare provider, insurance plan, government agency or employer has improperly disclosed personal medical information, though this did not usually cause them actual harm. Despite these experiences, most people still believe that the greatest threat to healthcare is the computerisation of medical records. There is much more concern about hackers breaking into systems than about authorised users leaking information.[13]

Although these surveys currently represent the best indicator of public attitudes toward medical privacy, they must be interpreted with caution, as responses to privacy-related surveys tend to be sensitive to the form and context of the questions.[14] Particular care also must be taken when interpreting American findings from a UK perspective, as the countries have very different privacy and healthcare regimes. In the USA, for example, it is not uncommon for an employer to act as its employees' health insurer, which significantly increases the potential for employees' medical information to be misused. This will obviously contribute to public concerns. There is also some doubt as to whether the American studies reflect current public attitudes, as they were mostly conducted before the commencement of the new medical privacy protections introduced by the US 'Privacy

---

* For example, those who had had pregnancy terminations or mental health problems were the most sensitive to routine sharing of information, whereas HIV-positive patients and those with genetic conditions were most concerned about the release of information outside the NHS.[11]

Rule'.* The effect of this Rule on public attitudes may be minimal, however, as it does not apply to all entities dealing with health information** and has come under a fair level of criticism. In any event, as the new regime only came into effect in April 2003, it is likely to be some time before its full impact is seen.

One area that is yet to be affected by rising concerns about medical privacy is litigation. Despite relatively high numbers of medical negligence actions, there have been very few court cases dealing with breaches of medical privacy.[15] This, however, does not necessarily indicate that the public is not concerned about this issue. More likely, it results from a number of different factors, such as the public being unaware of most of the unauthorised disclosures that take place, and individual patients not wanting to jeopardise their relationship with the offending healthcare provider, or wanting to avoid their confidential information being further disseminated during the complaint hearing. Consequently, the dearth of formal privacy complaints should not be used as an indicator of public attitudes.

Is there an increased threat to medical privacy?

In 1997 the US National Committee on Vital and Health Statistics reported that 'the United States is in the midst of a health privacy crisis'.[16] In the same year, the Caldicott Committee[17] in the UK concluded that there was a culture in the NHS of breaching patient privacy. Of the 86 different flows of personally identifiable data it found, 31 were not considered fully justified. Despite the implementation of both legal and policy changes since that time, the Office of the Data Protection Commissioner (now the Information Commissioner) has warned that the NHS is continuing to breach patient confidentiality, in violation of the Data Protection Act.[18] As concerning as these findings are, it is unclear whether they reflect an actual rise in the misuse of health data or simply a greater awareness of an existing problem.

---

*The Standards for Privacy of Individually Identifiable Health Information ('The Privacy Rule'), enacted under the Health Insurance Portability and Accountability Act 1996, establishes a set of national standards for the protection of certain health information. Most entities covered by the Rule were required to comply with the new requirements from 14 April 2003 (Privacy Rule, 45 CFR Section 164.534 (2002)).

**The 'Privacy Rule' regulates the use and disclosure of individually identifiable health information by covered entities. 'Covered entities' are health plans, healthcare clearing houses, and those healthcare providers who conduct certain financial and administrative transactions, such as enrolment and billing, electronically (Privacy Rule, 45 CFR Parts 160 and 164 (2002)).

Changes in the last few years have both increased and decreased the threat to information privacy. Living in an information age, where information itself is a valuable commodity, there is a greater financial incentive than ever before for breaching patient confidentiality. Equally, as discussed in Chapter 1, the range of people who have legitimate claims to access personal health data has grown significantly in recent years, with care being provided through medical teams. The number of secondary uses of health data has also risen.[19] This increase is due to a number of factors, such as conducting new types of research, greater emphasis being placed on accountability and monitoring of hospitals' performances, increased levels of litigation leading to more medical records being accessed through compulsory processes, and the emergence of new users of information, such as medical suppliers and pharmaceutical companies. In the USA it is estimated that 150 people will access the medical record of a single hospital patient.[20] Added to this is the fact that much more information is now recorded about patients, some of which, like genetic data and HIV status, is particularly sensitive.

Counterbalancing these developments is a marked increase in the emphasis placed on protecting the privacy of personal information, as evidenced by new legislative and policy initiatives throughout the world. Even critics of the current UK Data Protection Act would agree that it goes further than any of its predecessors toward protecting individuals' privacy. Although the NHS is yet to bring all of its practices into line with the requirements of the Act, improvements have been, and continue to be, seen, and patients at least now have a clear basis upon which to make complaints. The government's commitment to protecting patient privacy in the planned NHS restructuring is also a step in the right direction, although it remains to be seen how effectively this is implemented.[21]

One of the most important changes in the management of medical records in recent years has been the increased use of technology, which has led to a rise in the electronic storage and transmission of medical data, and to the development of electronic health records. These changes have had a mixed effect on health data security, having the potential to both increase and reduce privacy threats. Many patients are sceptical of the security and reliability of electronic databases, in particular they have significant anxieties because of the ability to retrieve and transfer immense amounts of information in very little time, often without the user having to be physically present at the hospital. These databases also enable different sets of information about an individual to be combined quickly and easily, potentially revealing new details about a patient or uncovering a previously anonymous patient's identity.

However, contrary to many people's fears, electronic medical records need not be more vulnerable than paper files to security breaches. Whilst it is true that most electronic record systems are not designed to protect completely against all unauthorised access, as this would make the system very costly and significantly reduce its usability, most systems do incorporate effective security measures. In such systems the risk of unauthorised access is very low, arguably lower than with paper records. Indeed, unlike paper records, computers can also restrict the amount of information that can be accessed by each legitimate user and can generate, automatically, access audit trails that can be used to detect (and therefore deter) improper practices. Further information about the impact of technology on patient privacy is provided in Chapter 4.

Although it is difficult to assess whether the privacy of medical information is really under more threat today than ever before, it is clear that many people perceive this to be the case. This may be largely attributable to patients' limited awareness of what happens to their data. According to an NHS Information Authority study,[11] patients have relatively poor understanding of the way their information is used in the NHS, many not having questioned confidentiality before taking part in the survey. For example, the majority of patients assumed that there was a much higher level of electronic information-sharing than actually exists. When patients do not understand what is done with their information they do not feel as if they have control over its use. It is this that tends to lead to fear and suspicion.[14] Whether justified or not, these feelings have the potential to affect the functioning of the health system and the success of new health initiatives. Public attitudes, therefore, as indicators of the opinions of individuals, cannot be ignored.

What are the risks of privacy breaches?

The misuse of health information can have a devastating effect on patients. Most immediately, it can cause substantial embarrassment and distress, and reduce patients' trust in healthcare providers. The disclosure of health information may also damage patients' sense of security and self-confidence, or cause them to be treated less favourably within the NHS.[22] This in turn may affect their decision to seek medical help, or to be fully candid with health professionals in the future. If patients fabricate or withhold information they may receive an incorrect diagnosis or be subjected to unnecessary tests, potentially causing them further pain and suffering, and placing their health at risk. Failure to report health problems, and providing incorrect or incomplete information also reduces the reliability of the data available for research, planning and public health reporting.[12]

Depending upon who obtains knowledge of the information, the unauthorised disclosure of identifiable current or future health information can also have economic consequences for patients. It may affect their ability to obtain health or life insurance, to find and hold employment or career advancements, to obtain housing or a mortgage, or to secure an education.[23] In some cases, the damage to a patient's reputation caused by the disclosure of health information may not only be humiliating, but may also have direct financial consequences.

For healthcare providers, the most obvious consequence of breaching patient privacy is legal liability or disciplinary action by the relevant professional body. Healthcare professionals who are concerned about their institution's privacy practices may also be tempted to keep separate, personal notes or to accede to patients' requests to omit information from their medical records. Both of these practices could cause problems for future treatment or in an emergency situation.

Do concerns affect behaviour?

Although there is a clear risk that failing to protect the privacy of medical data will cause patients to avoid treatment, or to conceal or fabricate information, there is little hard evidence that this actually occurs. The research that is available is mostly based on public opinion polls,[24] though what people believe they would do and what they actually do are often very different. For example, despite rating privacy as important, many people are willing to trade it quite cheaply, such as to earn points on store loyalty cards or for the chance to win prizes.[25] The difficulty of assessing the effect of privacy fears on behaviour is increased further by the fact that most of the relevant research has been conducted in the USA.

Although there are many reports about the effect poor privacy protection is having on behaviour, these are often based on questionable interpretations of research findings. An example of this is the review, by the Health Privacy Project at Georgetown University in the USA, of a 1999 independent US survey that found that one in seven adults said they had done something out of the ordinary to keep personal medical information confidential,[13] such as withholding information from their healthcare provider, providing inaccurate information, 'doctor hopping' to avoid the creation of a consolidated medical record and using their own funds for treatment covered by insurance. The Health Privacy Project concluded from this that 'people are afraid that their personal health information can be used against them and they are taking dramatic steps to protect their privacy'.[12] By contrast, the original researchers interpreted the results as showing that, although Americans are concerned about privacy, 'these concerns are having only a limited effect on the way they interact with the health care system'.[26]

Research conducted by the NHS Information Authority also suggests that patients' concerns about privacy may not always be reflected in their behaviour.[11] Although most patients had reservations about the privacy of electronic medical records and were keen to have the option to place selected information in a 'virtual sealed envelope' to which they could control access, few thought they would actually make use of this privacy measure. Sixty per cent of the participants said they would not want to put any information in it, with only 8% thinking they would fill it with a lot or all of their information. Importantly, however, most patients still wanted the envelope to exist. If the virtual envelope system is developed, monitoring the extent to which it is actually used may provide further insights into the way in which privacy concerns affect behaviour.

Until such information is available, it remains unclear whether there is a real connection between privacy fears and behaviour in the medical context. There is, however, significant concern among patients about the way their medical information is used and disclosed, which, whether justified or not, could affect the effectiveness and efficiency of the health system. These concerns cannot be ignored.

Summary

- The UK public is concerned about medical privacy, but generally trusts that doctors and the NHS will keep their medical records confidential.
- The privacy of health information is threatened in many different ways, though some of these are more likely to harm patients than others.
- A number of changes in the health sector, such as the delivery of treatment through medical teams, greater use of health information for secondary purposes, and increased use of computers, have heightened the threat to medical record privacy. At the same time, privacy protection has also improved through the introduction of more comprehensive privacy laws and policies.
- Breaches of medical privacy can cause emotional and financial damage to the patient, and lead to legal liability for the healthcare provider.
- It is unclear whether patients' privacy concerns actually cause them to change their behaviour. Despite this, these concerns must be addressed, as they will affect the extent to which the health system can operate effectively and efficiently.

References

1 Committee on Maintaining Privacy and Security in Healthcare Applications of the National Information Infrastructure, National Research Council (1997) *For the Record: protecting electronic health information.* National Academy Press, Washington DC.

2 Linowes D (1997) A Research Survey of Privacy in the Workplace. Unpublished White Paper, available from the University of Illinois at Urbana-Champaign.

3 (2003) Medical records found on memory stick. *E-Health Insider.* 12 March. (www.e-health-media.com/news/item/cfm?ID=383). (Accessed 7 July 2003.)

4 (1995) Hospital clerk's child allegedly told patients that they had AIDS. *Washington Post.* 1 March: A17.

5 Ernst and Young (2001) *The Health Industry and Privacy.* (www.ey.com/global/Content.nsf/Australia/AABS_-_TSRS_-_The_Health_Industry_and_Privacy). (Accessed 30 May 2003.)

6 Wahlberg D (1999) Patient records on web 2 months. *Ann Arbor News.* 11 February.

7 Lavelle M (1994) Health plan debate turning to privacy: some call for safeguards on medical disclosure. Is a federal law necessary? *National Law Journal.* 30 May: 1.

8 Needham K (2003) Watchdog barking over privacy lapses. *Sydney Morning Herald.* 7 January.

9 Australian Privacy Commissioner (1995) *Community Attitudes to Privacy,* Information Paper No. 3. Human Rights and Equal Opportunities Commission, Sydney.

10 Office of the Information Commissioner (2001) *Annual Report.* Office of the Information Commissioner, Sydney.

11 NHS Information Authority, The Consumers' Association, Health Which? (2002) *Share with Care – people's views on consent and confidentiality of patient information.* (www.nhsia.nhs.uk/confidentiality/pages/docs/swc.pdf). (Accessed 20 August 2003.)

12 Health Privacy Project (1999) *Exposed: a health privacy primer for consumers.* Institute for Health Care Research and Policy, Georgetown University. (www.healthprivacy.org/usr_doc/33806/pdf). (Accessed 10 March 2003.)

13 California Health Care Foundation (1999) *Americans Worry About the Privacy of their Computerised Medical Records.* (www.chcf.org/press/view.cfm?itemID=12267). (Accessed 10 March 2003.)

14 Performance and Innovation Unit (2002) *Privacy and Data Sharing: the way forward for public services.* (www.number-10.gov.uk/su/privacy/index.htm). (Accessed 30 October 2003.)

15 Chester M (2000) Patients' expectations and experiences (ACHCEW contribution). In: *Privacy in the Electronic NHS.* (Debate organised by the British

Medical Informatics Society, London, 30 November 2000.) (www.bmis.org/privacy2000/chester.doc). (Accessed 10 April 2003.)

16 National Committee on Vital and Health Statistics (1997) *Health Privacy and Confidentiality Recommendations*. (www.ncvhs.hhs.gov/privrecs.htm). (Accessed 10 April 2003.)

17 The Caldicott Committee (1997) *Report on the Review of Patient-identifiable Information*. NHS Executive. (www.doh.gov.uk/ipu/confiden/report/index. htm). (Accessed 5 August 2003.)

18 Cambridge Health Informatics Limited (2001) *Gaining Patient Consent to Disclosure*. (www.doh.gov.uk/ipu/confiden/gpcd/exec/gpcdexec.pdf). (Accessed 13 March 2003.)

19 Institute of Medicine (1994) *Health Data in the Information Age*. National Academy Press, Washington DC.

20 Goldman J and Choy A (2002) *Privacy and Confidentiality in Health Research*. The Online Ethics Center for Engineering and Science, Case Western Reserve University. (http://onlineethics.org/reseth/nbac/hgoldman.html#f3). (Accessed 30 May 2003.)

21 Department of Health (DoH) (2000) *The NHS Plan*. (www.doh.gov.uk/nhsplan/ index.htm). (Accessed 15 March 2003.)

22 Medical Research Council (2000) *Personal Information in Medical Research*. (Updated January 2003.) (www.mrc.ac.uk/pdf-pimr.pdf).

23 Cushman F and Detmer D (1998) Information policy for the US health sector: engineering, political economy and ethics. *Milbank Quarterly Special Edition Electronic Article*, January. (www.milbank.org/art). (Accessed 5 September 2003.)

24 Detmer D (2000) Your privacy or your health – will medical privacy legislation stop quality health care? *International Journal for Quality in Health Care*. **12**: 1.

25 Hawker A (2001) *Privacy as an Investment*. Security, Legal Issues and Confidentiality Special Interest Group, Birmingham Business School. (www.bham.ac.uk/ business/health/cba01.htm). (Accessed 15 April 2003.)

26 California Health Care Foundation (1999) *Medical Privacy and Confidentiality Survey*. (www.chcf.org/documents/ihealth/survey.pdf). (Accessed 10 March 2003.)

Chapter 3

Is consent the answer?

Freedom of choice is an important right in the modern world. Within certain legal parameters, individuals have the right to make their own decisions about most aspects of their lives. A key concept in maintaining this freedom is consent. Many activities would be considered illegal, and agreements unenforceable, except for the fact that the participants had provided their consent.

In healthcare, consent is crucial. Patients have the right to make their own decisions about the treatment they will receive and, except in emergency or extraordinary situations, it is illegal to attempt to treat patients without their consent. Provided they are competent to make the decision, patients even have the right to go against medical advice and refuse life-saving treatment. Not uncommonly the question of consent is at the heart of medical negligence claims, in particular whether a patient was given enough information to provide valid consent and whether the procedure went beyond the scope of that consent.

Given the important role consent plays in the delivery of healthcare, it is not surprising that it is being favoured as a means of regulating the way in which medical records are used, with both professional and patient groups supporting this approach. The General Medical Council, for example, advises doctors to seek patients' consent, wherever possible, before disclosing their information, even if they do not believe that a patient can be identified from it.[1] Consent is also the approach currently favoured by the government, having been highlighted as a key factor for dealing with privacy in the planned NHS restructuring.[2,3] This option also seems to appeal to most patients, as the right to give and withhold consent increases patients' sense of control over, and involvement in, their healthcare.[4]

Using consent to regulate the use of medical records offers many benefits. It overcomes the problem that different people have very different attitudes about the use of their health information, and gives credibility to the modern view of healthcare as being driven by patient needs. If implemented properly, consent will not only protect healthcare providers from legal liability, but also increase patients' trust in health professionals, leading to more information-sharing and better medical treatment. By contrast, patients who do not feel they have control over the use of their information, be that due to lack of knowledge, choice or the ability to check that their wishes are upheld, may take their own steps to protect their privacy, such as withholding information during treatment. The likelihood of this happening is discussed in Chapter 2.

Despite these potential benefits, it is quite difficult to formulate an effective consent model that can cope with the many complex issues that arise in practice. In trying to develop a workable model, policy makers are faced with a range of difficult questions, such as how specific the consent needs to be, how it should be obtained, and the circumstances in which it is appropriate to override a refusal. Whether a consent-based approach to medical record management is ultimately beneficial for patients depends, to a large extent, upon how it is put into practice; specifically, the type of information provided to patients, how well it is understood, the degree of choice patients have, or feel they have, and the extent to which that choice is respected.

How does consent fit into the Data Protection Act 1998?

There is no express requirement in the Data Protection Act 1998 for healthcare providers to obtain consent before using or disclosing a patient's health information. Consent is, however, indirectly required by the obligation, in the first data protection principle, to process information lawfully. As discussed in Box 3.1, processing lawfully requires that healthcare providers comply with all relevant statutes and common law rules. This includes the duty of confidentiality, which prevents doctors (and many other health professionals) using confidential information disclosed within the doctor–patient relationship for any purpose other than that for which it was provided, without patients' agreement.* Save for in a few exceptional circumstances (for example, patient information can be disclosed without consent where it is justified by some overriding public interest or the disclosure is allowed under regulations made under the Health and Social Care Act 2000, Section 60), healthcare providers will therefore need to obtain patients' consent before using their information for purposes unrelated to patients' medical care.[1] Obviously, the healthcare provider must ensure that this consent is valid and enforceable.

---

*C v C (1946) 1 All ER 562.

Box 3.1

Lawful processing of information

The first and second data protection principles in the Data Protection Act 1998 impose the main restrictions on the collection and use of personal information.

First data protection principle:

> *Personal data shall be processed fairly and lawfully and, in particular, shall not be processed unless*
> - *at least one of the conditions in Schedule 2 is met; and*
> - *in the case of sensitive personal data, at least one of the conditions in Schedule 3 is also met.*

As information about a person's physical or mental health is classified as sensitive personal data, whenever such information is collected, used or disclosed the healthcare provider or other entity doing so must ensure that:

- The processing is fair – although what constitutes fair processing will depend on the specific circumstances, the principal consideration is the effect processing will have on the interests of the patient. As part of the requirement to process data fairly, the patient must be given certain details, called fair processing information, at the time the data is collected, informing them of the identity of the data controller, the purpose or purposes for which the information is being collected and any other information considered necessary. For example, it may be necessary to inform them of the consequences of collection if this is not otherwise apparent.
- The processing is lawful – this means that the collection, use and disclosure of the data must be in accordance with all applicable laws. For healthcare providers the most relevant law is the common law duty of confidentiality, which is enshrined in most health professional codes of conduct.
- One of the conditions in each of schedules 2 and 3 is satisfied – in the healthcare sector, it is usually quite easy to comply with this requirement as most processing of information will be covered by:
  - a number of conditions in Schedule 2, such as the processing being done with consent, being necessary to protect the patient's vital interests, or being necessary for the purposes of the healthcare

provider's legitimate interests (and not prejudicial to the patient's rights or freedoms); and
– the Schedule 3 condition that the processing is necessary for medical purposes and is undertaken by a health professional or someone with an equivalent duty of confidentiality. 'Medical purposes' is defined quite widely in the Act to include preventative medicine, medical diagnosis, medical research, the provision of care and treatment and the management of healthcare services.

Second data protection principle:
Personal data shall be obtained only for one or more specified and lawful purposes, and shall not be further processed in any manner incompatible with that purpose or those purposes.

This prevents a healthcare provider using information for any new purpose, other than that communicated to the patient at the time the information was collected, without obtaining the patient's permission.

What is required for valid consent?

There are three basic requirements for consent to be valid.[5] First, before making their choice, patients must be given sufficient information about the activities to which they are being asked to consent and the consequences of their decision. In the context of medical records, this requires that patients are told, and understand, what part of their medical record is affected, to whom it will be disclosed, what the recipients will do with it, and the effect (if any) on themselves of both agreeing to, and refusing to allow, the disclosure. It is not necessary to tell patients things that they already know, but care should be taken when making assumptions about patients' levels of knowledge.

The second requirement is that the consent be given voluntarily. Armed with the knowledge needed to make an informed decision, patients must have a real choice as to whether or not they will agree to the proposed use or disclosure. Arguably, there is no such freedom of choice if withholding consent means that patients will be denied treatment, will face a significant increase in waiting time or will incur additional costs. The attitude of the staff member seeking consent may also cast doubt upon its validity if a patient, on reasonable grounds, feels pressured to comply.

The final requirement for valid consent is the existence of some mechanism to record and implement patients' decisions. There is no point going through the consent process if the particular record system does not have an adequate method of registering and updating patients' wishes, and ensuring that those wishes are made known to, and followed by, relevant personnel. This does not necessarily mean that a consent form must be signed, just that patients' wishes, be they expressed in writing, orally or by their actions, can be noted in their medical records in a way that will ensure that they are respected.

These basic requirements can be met in a range of ways, giving rise to several types of consent.

Express versus implied consent

As its name suggests, *express consent* requires individuals to indicate their agreement in some explicit manner. Although a written document can be useful evidence of what was agreed, particularly if it records the information given to a patient as well as the act of consent, it is equally acceptable for the background information or the actual consent to be provided orally. By contrast, *implied consent* is assumed to have been given when individuals take some action, such as participating in, or complying with, an activity, in the knowledge that doing so will indicate their consent to a particular occurrence. Rugby players, for example, do not commit assault every time they tackle an opposition player, as, by electing to play, that opponent is taken to have implied consent to the normal rough and tumble of the game. As with all consent, the decision to engage in the activity that gives rise to the implication of consent must be informed and voluntary.

The medical community currently relies heavily upon implied consent. Attendance at a doctor's surgery is usually accepted as sufficient indication that patients agree to a relevant examination. Equally, taking a general practitioner's referral to the radiography department demonstrates implied consent to undergoing an X-ray examination. Despite the apparent informal nature, implied consent is no less valid than its express counterpart, and is an acceptable way of providing consent for many of the purposes of the Data Protection Act 1998.[6] However, as express consent can be less ambiguous, the Information Commissioner has suggested that this may be a preferable way of obtaining consent where there is a substantial risk of misunderstanding.[7] This will often be the case when dealing with the future use of patient information, as many patients know little about the purposes for which medical records are used, and may be preoccupied with other health matters at the relevant time. The nature of the particular situation also may affect the risk of misunderstanding; relevant considerations being the type of information or disclosure involved, and the age, ethnicity, intellectual capacity and emotional state of the patient.

Specific versus general consent

Irrespective of how consent is obtained, it only authorises those activities that fall within its scope. Even where consent is worded fairly generally, there is usually some limit on the range of activities it covers. Defining this limit can be difficult.

In the case of implied consent, the scope is determined by reference to what people expected would occur when they engaged in the activity. A rugby player's participation in a match, for example, is likely to be considered sufficient grounds for implying his consent to being tackled, but this consent would not authorise the use of a weapon in a tackle, as this is not an expected consequence of playing. The status of an illegal, head-high tackle, however, or a post-tackle punch, is more difficult to determine, both being outside the rules of the game but reasonably common occurrences. Except in particularly severe cases, both acts would probably be included in the implied consent.

Even with express consent, where the covered activities are articulated in some way, a degree of judgement may still be required. As it is impractical, if not impossible, to list every single act that is included in a consent, patients are usually assumed also to agree to a range of ancillary activities that are necessary for, or a component of, the principal activity to which they consented. The ancillary activities within this category are those acts that both parties understood to be part of the consent. Consenting to the amputation of the left leg, for example, would not authorise the amputation of any other body part, but would cover activities that most people would know are necessary for the amputation operation to occur, such as the insertion of stitches.

To avoid the difficulties of defining the limits of consent, it is often tempting to draft consent forms in very general terms. Whilst theoretically it is possible for patients to consent to their doctors doing 'everything that he or she believes, for whatever reason, should be done to me' or to 'disclose my medical records to whomever, and for whatever reason, the doctor likes', not many patients would agree to this. Even if they did, it would not always have the intended effect. Despite the open-ended wording, if a disagreement arose about what could be done with the record, activities or disclosures that would have been outside patients' reasonable expectations usually will be considered beyond the scope of the consent. Obtaining a very wide consent also fails to achieve any of the other benefits of the consent process, such as giving patients a greater sense of security through increased understanding and control. For maximum protection to both doctors and patients the ideal breadth of consent is the somewhat unhelpful 'as specific as the circumstances reasonably allow'. The NHS Information Authority is currently developing a national consent form that may go a long way to solving some of the difficulties of determining the appropriate level of detail required. The guidance on drafting consent forms in Box 3.2 may be of assistance.

Box 3.2

Consent forms

Consent forms should:

- Be as brief as reasonably practicable (long, wordy documents are less likely to be read and more likely to cause confusion).
- Use clear, patient-friendly language, and no legal or medical jargon. Protecting the healthcare provider from legal liability is not the sole aim of the consent form.
- Clearly differentiate between uses and disclosures that are conditional upon receiving treatment and those that are truly optional.
- Minimise the extent to which healthcare providers or patients can insert their own words. Although it will not be possible to cover every eventuality, it is best to limit the use of categories such as 'other, please specify', as the information inserted may be inaccurate, unclear, ambiguous or overly specific or general. It will also result in each consent form differing slightly from the next.
- Describe the requested uses and disclosures as specifically as necessary for the majority of patients to be satisfied that they have sufficient information to make an informed decision. Being too specific will unduly restrict what can be done with medical records, whereas being too general will cause patients to either refuse to provide consent or insist on further, personalised restrictions. Testing draft consent forms on real patient groups may help to identify the appropriate level of detail.

Although the validity of consent is not altered by the passage of time, it is advisable to check periodically that patients' wishes, concerning the use of their medical data, have not changed. It is unreasonable to assume that consent preferences remain unchanged when a person's circumstances have altered considerably.[8] Although it would usually be unnecessarily time-consuming and cumbersome to check consent at every consultation, healthcare providers should prompt patients to review their consent preferences after a number of years or after a significant change in the patient's medical condition.

What is done in the UK?

The NHS uses patients' medical records for a wide range of purposes, many of which are not directly connected to patients' care and treatment. The NHS usually relies upon implied consent to do this, a great deal of which is not valid and is therefore open to legal challenge. Implied consent is often used, for example, to justify the disclosure of personal information for clinical audits, research, financial audits and NHS management decisions, despite the fact that most patients are unaware that their records are used in these ways. According to the Information Commissioner, the NHS currently is not giving patients sufficient information about the way in which it uses their medical records, which is creating a vast gap between patients' expectations and NHS practice.[5] By failing to provide this information to patients, and then by using and disclosing patients' personal information without valid consent, the NHS is operating in breach of the Data Protection Act 1998.

The implied consent relied upon by the NHS may also be invalid because of the failure to make patients aware of their right to object to their records being disclosed or to give them an opportunity to exercise that right. In any event, attempts to object to particular disclosures often would be unsuccessful, as many of the current processes and technologies employed by the NHS are unable to support such a decision.[5] The Information Commissioner's opinion on current NHS practice is considered in more detail later in this chapter.

What type of consent is best in a medical context?

The Data Protection Act 1998 and doctors' duty of confidentiality to their patients provide the legal framework for requiring consent, but neither set of laws gives clear guidance on the type of consent required or how it should be obtained.

Express, written consent, usually via a consent form, is often seen as providing the greatest protection for both patients and healthcare providers. In theory at least, the consent form draws patients' attention to the fact that their medical records will be used for a variety of purposes, clarifies the types of disclosures being requested, and provides evidence of patients' decisions. By having to read and sign the form, patients are given a clear opportunity to make their objections known.

Obtaining express consent for all uses of patient information, however, is a very expensive and time-consuming undertaking, involving much more than simply printing a few forms. Attempting to do this would cost the NHS approximately £400 million,* which includes the cost of:

- changing NHS processes to ensure that the existence of express consent is checked and to enable refusals to be respected
- contacting existing patients to obtain instructions for data that have already been collected (this will be a sizeable administrative task, given the likelihood that many contact details will have changed and follow-up letters usually will be required to elicit a response from many people. It has been estimated that it could take up to seven mailings to obtain more than a 50% response rate).[5]
- constantly updating the consents as new flows of data arise, patients change their minds, and legislation and policies are altered.

Even if the necessary money and time were invested, it would not be possible to contact and obtain a response from every patient. Where a response is not received, patients must be assumed to have refused their consent or else the process simply becomes an expensive form of implied consent. The disadvantage of this assumption is that a low response rate will result in large numbers of patients having been deemed to have refused their consent, which in turn will affect the quality of data available for research, audits and planning. Although this approach gives patients a lot of control over their personal privacy, it also requires a heavy investment of financial and staff resources and is likely to cause a decline in data quality. Express consent models have been successfully adopted by some of the demonstrator communities in the Electronic Record Development and Implementation Programme (ERDIP),** but these only involved small patient samples. Consequently, their experiences may not be scaleable to entire NHS trusts.

The cost and difficulty of requiring express consent for all uses of medical records has led many commentators to prefer a model that relies mostly on valid, implied consent, with express consent only needed for more contentious uses, such as those that are likely to affect patients directly or that require a lengthy explanation. By limiting express consent to uses that are most likely to raise concern for a reasonable number of patients, overall costs

---

* The £400 million estimate is based upon the approximate costs of sending letters and forms to the 60 million members of the public, returning those letters, sending multiple follow-ups, and carrying out the necessary data entry and validation. The estimate includes the cost of follow-ups every five years, but not the cost of initially changing the NHS processes.

** ERDIP is a programme developed by the NHS Information Authority to develop and demonstrate in real clinical settings how electronic health records can be used to share patients' information across health and social care communities. This is principally done through in-service practical work by ERDIP demonstrator communities. For further information *see*: www.nhsia.nhs.uk/erdip/pages/default.asp.

are reduced. This approach, which is supported by the NHS Information Authority,[2] strikes a balance between privacy, on the one hand, and cost and inconvenience, on the other.

The draft confidentiality code of practice for NHS staff,[3] currently being developed by the Department of Health, also favours a model relying on a combination of implied and express consent, but requires express consent in a wider range of circumstances. Under this Code, implied consent is only acceptable for information-sharing that is necessary for the provision of healthcare, such as providing treatment, conducting clinical audits and to share information with children's parents. Disclosures for non-healthcare purposes, such as research, financial audits, health service management, epidemiology and to hospital chaplains, requires express consent, which must be recorded either in a consent form or as a note in the medical record. To obtain express consent, the Code requires that patients be informed of the information being recorded, the ways in which it will be used, the benefits of agreeing to the sharing, how the information will be protected (including how long it will be retained and how it will be destroyed), the outcomes and risks if consent is withheld and whether consent can be withdrawn later.

It is likely that the Information Commissioner will uphold these types of models, having indicated that implied consent is acceptable in the medical context provided that the fair processing of information required by the Data Protection Act 1998 is given at an appropriate time and patients accept treatment without objecting to any uses or disclosures.[7] In other words, implied consent is acceptable provided it is informed and voluntary, and the requirements of the Data Protection Act 1998 are followed. The Information Commissioner did, however, suggest that express consent may be required on some occasions, such as where the fair processing of information was not given because the data was collected before the Data Protection Act was enacted, or because the purpose for which it is to be processed has changed since collection. This guidance, however, only relates to the minimum requirements of the Data Protection Act 1998, which do not necessarily accord with good practice. Healthcare providers must also consult relevant guidelines written by government bodies and professional groups, as these will be considered by the Information Commissioner when deciding whether express or implied consent is required in specific circumstances.

How should the information be given?

One of the main difficulties with using consent, either express or implied, to regulate the use of medical records is finding a cost-effective and efficient method of providing sufficient information to patients about the way in which their records will be used, to enable them to make an informed decision. As the target audience for this information is effectively the entire UK population, it would be economically and administratively impossible to do this via individual letters. Much more cost-effective is making this information available through NHS establishments, such as during consult-ations or in leaflets and posters in waiting rooms.

Although this approach will only reach those people who use NHS services, obtaining consent from these people will actually cover quite a large proportion of the patient data held by the NHS. Obviously, it will cover all new information collected, as such data can only be obtained from current NHS users. It will also cover a large percentage of the data that has already been collected, as approximately 80% of the population uses the NHS in any one year.[5] The only data unaccounted for, therefore, is that previously collected about the remaining 20% of the population. One way of dealing with this problem is to exclude this data from research and audit activities, and from other secondary uses, on the basis that consent to such uses cannot be implied. Doing so, however, may have a significant effect on the results obtained, as NHS attendance rates are not uniform across all socio-demographic sectors, with elderly people and young children being over-represented. The excluded 20% of the population is therefore likely to include disproportionate numbers of certain groups, such as adults of working age.

For this reason, it is probably necessary to use a host of different communication methods, each delivering different levels of information. This type of approach is recommended by NHS Scotland[9] and in the report for the NHS Executive prepared by Cambridge Health Informatics,[5] and has also received support from the Information Commissioner.

The first level of information, suggested by both NHS Scotland and Cambridge Health Informatics, is a public awareness campaign about medical record privacy, delivered through the mass media.* Although, with the NHS being a national body, it seems sensible to conduct this as a national campaign, locally run initiatives can foster a greater sense of immediacy for the community, potentially increasing the effectiveness of the message transmitted. With this in mind, NHS Scotland has suggested that the mass media campaign be implemented through the development of a national toolkit through which local campaigns can be run.

Whether conducted locally or nationally, this method of communication will not, on its own, satisfy the requirements of the Data Protection Act 1998, as it is only able to provide a very limited amount of information. What it will

---

*NHS Scotland also considered the possibility of achieving this through a household mail drop.

do, however, is provide basic awareness and understanding of the issues, preparing patients for the receipt of further details. It will also make those patients with real privacy concerns aware of their right to obtain further information.

The next level of information can be provided through the distribution of a variety of leaflets and booklets, some directed at patients generally and others addressing data-sharing practices relating to specific conditions and treatments. To ensure there is some consistency in the information disclosed by different NHS organisations, whilst maintaining sufficient flexibility to allow for organisational differences, NHS Scotland recommends that the leaflets be developed by the Department of Health, but delivered in electronic form, thus enabling them to be altered easily. The Cambridge Health Informatics report provides a detailed examination of the type of information that should be provided in the leaflets and other materials; this is summarised in Box 3.3.

Box 3.3

Method of informing patients proposed by Cambridge Health Informatics

The Cambridge Health Informatics report[5] recommends different levels of detail be provided in different ways.

- At the most general level, patients are to be made aware of the issues involved in medical record confidentiality and use, through mass media advertisements and posters in NHS establishments. Through these media patients are to be informed that information provided to the NHS is kept confidential, but is used for purposes in addition to direct healthcare. Patients will be reminded that this is important for everyone's healthcare, but that individuals have the right to object to how their information is used and can seek further information.

- At the next level, known as the 'general information' stage, further details are provided through patient leaflets. An example of the information provided at this level is the knowledge that records will be used for 'research purposes'. Although Cambridge Health Informatics believes that this level of detail is sufficient for consent to be properly implied for most purposes, it is questionable whether the description 'research purposes' gives patients enough information to enable them to make an informed decision about what will happen to their data. The assumption is that patients who are concerned about privacy in research or the types of research that could take place can seek further information. Whether this works in practice depends to a large degree on the culture and staff attitudes of each organisation, and patients' trust in the NHS.

- In addition, more detailed leaflets will be available explaining further information-sharing practices that may apply to particular activities or illnesses. For example, cancer leaflets will inform patients that their information will be recorded in a cancer database that is shared with the National Cancer Registry, to help to try and understand and treat the disease. The report suggests that this level of information is required before consent can be implied to a disclosure that could cause detriment to the patient, but points out that as little more effort is required by this stage to go the next step and obtain express consent, this may be a preferable route for potentially detrimental disclosures.
- Lastly, more detailed information also will be available to patients upon request.

Providing detailed information in written form has a lot of merit. It ensures that each patient receives the same basic information and gives patients an opportunity to digest it and consider their decision; it reduces the workload of front-line staff; and it provides a record of at least some of the information patients received. However, care must be taken to ensure such information is accessible to non-English speakers and those with poor literacy skills or disabilities that make reading or comprehending difficult.* It is also essential that the information in these leaflets and booklets is clear and correct, providing a sufficient level of detail, but not overloading patients with information or raising unnecessary alarm.

Irrespective of their quality, providing leaflets and other written material should only ever be considered as one step in the consent-seeking process. For leaflets to be an acceptable method of communication it is crucial that staff ensure that patients not only obtain a copy of the leaflet but also that they understand its contents. This can be done by reception staff, healthcare providers, or a combination of the two. As the way in which this is carried out will heavily influence patients' understanding of the information, and affect their confidence about raising concerns or queries, the culture of the organisation and the attitude of staff members is critical. Despite an abundance of written materials and verbal explanations, many patients will still be confused about their rights and the information-sharing to which

---

* This could account for a significant number of people as it is estimated that 22% of the UK population is functionally illiterate, though the research supporting this claim has been criticised on methodological grounds.[10]

they are agreeing unless they feel comfortable about voicing their concerns. Ensuring this requires staff members not only to invite questions but also to be positive about receiving them, and to have the time and knowledge to provide useful answers, or at least direct patients toward more appropriate sources. Any perception that staff do not have the time or inclination to provide further information is likely to deter questions, except from the most assertive patients.

The potential for this aspect of the consent-seeking process to be overlooked is well illustrated by the varying experiences of the hospitals participating in the ERDIP pilot studies, each of which placed different emphasis on the need to ensure that patients understood the information they received. The information-sharing protocol used in central Hampshire, for example, restricted consent-seeking to those staff trained in the appropriate procedures. It stressed that patients must be given sufficient time to consider the material and to fully digest and understand their rights. It did not, however, define what length of time would be considered sufficient, as this would depend on the types of disclosures requested and on patients' intellectual capacity and emotional state.

In contrast, the protocol developed by the West Surrey Health Community focused almost entirely on the need to record the fact that an information leaflet was provided to patients and that consent was given, rather than on the importance of ensuring that patients understood the leaflets. This approach makes it more likely that the provision of information will be seen as something that is done in order to tick a box, not as an aid to equipping patients with the knowledge they need to make an informed decision.

The Department of Health's confidentiality code of practice for NHS staff[3] also recognises the need to ensure that patients actually understand the information they receive. It stresses the importance of checking, both at the reception desk and during actual consultations, that patients have seen and understood leaflets, that they are aware of their choices and have no concerns. It also advises clinicians to inform patients whenever information is recorded in their medical record. Although this may seem onerous, with practice, phrases such as *'Let me note that in your file'* can be integrated into normal consultation discussions.

Given the important role played by front-line staff in all of the communication strategies discussed above, informing patients about the ways their medical records are used and disclosed is likely to involve significant staff time and effort. Although this can be reduced by integrating the provision of information into existing processes, there are fears that the demands of informed consent on front-line staff have not been considered properly.[11] Although the ERDIP pilot studies provided little concrete evidence about the staff resources involved in obtaining either express or implied consent, consent issues were a common source of problems.[12] Based on its experience, the Walsall demonstrator site predicted that compliance with the requirements of patient consent would have a 'significant impact' on the organisations involved, and that over the course of a day 'the overall time impact on clinicians may be considerable'.[13] The experiences of the ERDIP communities have prompted a call for the creation of a new healthcare position, the 'clinical information support worker', employed to assist patients in understanding consent issues and making their decisions.[12] It may also be beneficial to involve front-line staff in developing consent-seeking protocols.

Staff time will also be consumed by the fact that if patients do ask questions and request further information before providing their consent, the scope of that consent may need to be restricted in accordance with the additional information provided. For example, if, following concerns about disclosures for 'research purposes', patients are given further details about the nature of the research or the bodies conducting it, their consent must be assumed to be restricted to that area or those bodies, as the case may be, unless they expressly state otherwise. To ensure that this occurs, there must be some method of auditing and confirming the way individuals' information is used. It is also important to ensure, as far as possible, that the additional information provided to different patients on request is consistent. Significant administrative problems could arise if the delivery of slightly different information to each patient seeking clarification results in them each having their own, very specific, range of consent. If requests for further information are common, it may be best to increase the level of detail provided to all patients initially.

From the above discussion it is clear that there is no ideal approach for communicating detailed information to the entire population. However, by relying on a variety of different communication methods the limitations of the individual ones become less critical. The time commitment required from front-line staff, however, should not be underestimated.

Can consent be a condition of treatment?

As we have seen, consent is only valid if patients have a real choice about the decisions they make. A right to object to a particular disclosure ceases to be much of a right at all if refusal results in the denial of treatment. The consent may not be considered to be truly voluntary and will therefore not be enforceable. Some information-sharing, however, such as between members of the patients' healthcare teams, is essential for the proper and efficient delivery of medical treatment. Can the provision of treatment therefore be made conditional upon patients consenting to such disclosures?

According to the Information Commissioner, this is an acceptable practice for uses of information that are essential to the provision of healthcare.[7] The Information Commissioner identified a number of these uses, including:

- the provision of care and treatment
- routine record keeping
- the provision of treatment in medical emergencies
- conducting clinical audits, which are used to monitor the standard of care provided to patients
- carrying out essential administrative activities, such as those that allow general practitioners to obtain payment for treatment they provided
- conducting administrative audits, which are used to determine funding allocation and other matters to improve the efficiency of the NHS.

The Information Commissioner's guidelines recognise that the patient's position as the controller of his or her information must sometimes give way to the legitimate needs of a modern health service. This need not, however, have a major impact on patient privacy, as many of the activities in the list can be achieved by use of anonymous or pseudo-anonymous data, or at least by the disclosure of only limited amounts of identifying information. Merely because the Information Commissioner has recognised that certain uses of information are essential and can legitimately be made conditions of treatment does not authorise healthcare providers to disclose more information than is necessary, or to use personally identifying information where anonymous data will suffice.

It is important to note that the Information Commissioner's list does not include secondary uses of data, such as research, which, although unrelated to the direct provision of care, is important for medical advancement and health surveillance. This may reflect a belief by the Commissioner that, if treatment is to be made conditional upon patients agreeing to such uses, this is best achieved by specific legislation, and not by a liberal interpretation of the general data protection laws.

The Information Commissioner also recognises that, despite it being acceptable to make certain uses of information a condition of treatment, there will still be some circumstances where it is reasonable for patients to object. For example, if a patient personally knows a member of the administrative staff, a request that special arrangements be made in respect of record keeping and other such procedures should usually be respected. If the healthcare provider is unwilling to accommodate the patient's concerns, the patient can make a written objection under Section 10 of the Data Protection Act 1998 if the processing of his or her record is likely to cause unwarranted and substantial damage or distress.

Among the essential uses of information identified by the Information Commissioner is the consultation of medical records for care and treatment. As this is the primary reason medical records are created, patients normally would not be expected to object to their information being used for this purpose. The increasing use of medical teams in the provision of healthcare, however, means that 'use for treatment' can justify disclosure to a wide range of people, some of whom the patient may not have met. Although refusing to allow this disclosure could jeopardise the quality of care that can be provided, it should be the patient's decision whether they accept this risk. Although some healthcare providers may feel that giving patients this level of control impinges on their commitment to provide the best possible care they can, their duty as a health professional is fulfilled provided that patients understand the dangers associated with their decision.* As long as the withholding of consent is an informed decision by a competent person** that decision should be respected, in the same way as a competent person's refusal to undergo life-saving treatment.

The British Medical Association (BMA) recognises a competent person's right to refuse to allow information-sharing with other health professionals even where it may compromise patients' safety.[15] According to the BMA, 'individuals may knowingly compromise their own safety but not that of other people'.[15] However, it also recognises that doctors have a right to curtail the range of procedures offered if the outcome might foreseeably be unsafe or ineffective due to lack of information, provided the patient understands this.

Where treatment is conditional upon patients agreeing to certain uses of information, this fact must be explained clearly to them. Most importantly, the notification that these disclosures will take place should not be made to look like a request for consent. Requesting consent where patients can only prevent the disclosure by not obtaining treatment may make patients confused about their rights. They may also become sceptical about the consent process, coming to view all consent forms as meaningless and not worthy of proper consideration. In providing information to patients about

---

*In case a disagreement arises later, it is always advisable to document both patients' objections to the disclosure of their medical records and doctors' cautions against taking this stance.

** A person is considered competent if they can comprehend information (it having been presented in a clear way), believe it, and retain it long enough to weigh it up and make a decision (Re C (Adult: Refusal of Medical Treatment) (1994) 1 All ER 819). Adults are assumed to be competent unless it is demonstrated otherwise. A patient may be competent to make some decisions, but lack the capacity to make others. An unexpected decision does not mean that the patient is incompetent, but it may indicate that more information needs to be provided to them.[14] (The same view is expressed by the General Medical Council.)

the ways in which their medical records will be used, therefore, healthcare providers should clearly differentiate between disclosures that are required for treatment to be provided, and those that are truly optional.

Is consent really the issue?

Whilst consent, with its links to personal autonomy and freedom of choice, is an appealing way of regulating the use of patients' records, control is of little value without the knowledge and understanding needed to exercise it effectively. For the consent model to protect patients from damaging or distressing disclosures, patients must have a good understanding of the disclosures being contemplated. This will not always be the case.[16]

Even where healthcare providers have been transparent about how they use medical records, and patients have been given the opportunity to ask questions, they will often have little detailed understanding of the nature of these disclosures, the privacy and security policies that will be used to protect their information, or the extent to which these policies will be followed. With little or no knowledge or experience of hospital administration or research practices, many patients will have difficulty understanding the information with which they are presented. Some patients may deal with this problem by taking the most cautious, privacy-protecting stance, denying all access to their records that is not to their direct and obvious benefit. This works to the detriment of the wider society. Others will agree to disclosures despite their confusion and reservations. Neither scenario is appealing.

For this reason, it has been suggested that the emphasis on giving patients control may be somewhat misguided. Whilst freedom of choice will always be important, the real issue is not control of information but maintaining patients' dignity, which is achieved by protecting them from offensive and embarrassing disclosures.[16] The importance of protecting individuals who cannot protect themselves is the reason independent bodies, including the Information Commissioner, are needed, with powers not only to check that the privacy guidelines of individual organisations are adequate, but that they are actually being followed. Whilst accidental leaks to newspapers and the internet are 'headline-grabbing', the vast majority of breaches of privacy are of such a nature that they would not come to the attention of ordinary patients.

Although protecting dignity is clearly important, it is not an ideal basis for determining who should have access to medical records, as there will be substantial differences between the disclosures that individual patients find offensive or embarrassing.* Relying on consent, on the other hand, can accommodate these individual differences. In fact, the use of consent in medical record management ensures that responsibility for maintaining dignity is placed in patients' hands.

The concept of dignity may still be useful, however, as a guide to help healthcare providers and policy makers determine when it is appropriate to override patients' wishes about how their medical records should be used. The likely impact of a particular disclosure on a patient's dignity may be a relevant factor to consider when determining whether it is appropriate to release information against patients' wishes or without patients' knowledge. Although the concept of maintaining dignity is unlikely to replace consent as the main method of regulating access to medical records, therefore, it may be a relevant consideration in difficult situations.

Summary

- Regulating access to medical records through consent is a good way of dealing with the fact that patients have very different views about what uses and disclosures are acceptable.
- Consent can be:
  - *express* – less ambiguous but expensive and time-consuming, especially for previously collected data
  - *implied* – more efficient, acceptable for most purposes of the Data Protection Act 1998, but not always as certain as express consent.
- Most popular solution: valid implied consent for most uses, with express consent required for more contentious ones.
- Problem: devising a cost-effective method of providing sufficient information to patients to enable them to give their informed consent.
- Solution: providing different levels of detail through a number of different communication channels, including:
  - mass media
  - written information provided through the NHS (e.g. posters, leaflets, pamphlets)
  - additional information and clarification provided orally by reception staff and health professionals.

---

* There are, however, numerous examples of lawmakers, with or without public consultation, having legally enshrined a particular moral belief, without there being universal acceptance of the position taken. Drinking, voting and driving ages, for example, apply to all people, whether or not the ages chosen, or the existence of limits at all, accord with the individual's beliefs. The same is true for speed limits, euthanasia bans and the obligation to pay taxes.

References

1 General Medical Council (2000) *Confidentiality: protecting and providing information.* GMC, London.

2 NHS Information Authority (2002) *Caring for Information – model for the future.* (www.nhsia.nhs.uk/confidentiality/pages/consultation/docs/caring_model. pdf). (Accessed 8 July 2003.)

3 Department of Health (DoH) (2002) *Confidentiality: a code of practice for NHS staff (draft).* (www.nhsia.nhs.uk/confidentiality/page/consultation/docs/code_ prac.pdf). (Accessed 24 June 2003.)

4 NHS Information Authority, The Consumers' Association, Health Which? (2002) *Share with Care – people's views on consent and confidentiality of patient information.* (www.nhsia.nhs.uk/confidentiality/pages/docs/swc.pdf). (Accessed 20 August 2003.)

5 Cambridge Health Informatics Limited (2001) *Gaining Patient Consent to Disclosure.* (www.doh.gov.uk/ipu/confiden/gpcd/exec/gpcdexec.pdf). (Accessed 13 March 2003.)

6 Information Commissioner (1998) *Data Protection Act 1998: legal guidance.* Version 1. (www.dataprotection.gov.uk/dpr/dpdoc.nsf), under 'Legal Guidance'. (Accessed 30 March 2003.)

7 Information Commissioner (2002) *Use and Disclosure of Health Data.* (www.dataprotection.gov.uk/dpr/dpdoc.nsf), under 'Compliance Advice'. (Accessed 10 May 2003.)

8 Department of Health (DoH) (2002) *Legal and Policy Constraints on Electronic Records: options.* (www.nhsia.nhs.uk/erdip/pages/evaluation/docs/ consentconfid/legal%20and%20policy%20constraints%20Requirements %20Report%20v11.pdf). (Accessed 5 May 2003.)

9 Confidentiality and Security Advisory Group for Scotland (2002) *Protecting Patient Confidentiality – final report.* Scottish Executive Health Department. (www.show.scot.nhs.uk/sehd/publications/ppcr/ppcr.pdf). (Accessed 6 August 2003.)

10 Organisation for Economic Co-operation and Development (OECD) (2000) *Literacy in the Age of Information.* (www1.oecd.org/publications.e-book/ 8100051e.pdf). (Accessed 10 May 2003.)

11 NHS Information Authority (2002) *Tees ERDIP Demonstrator Programme, Project 3 – consent and confidentiality.* (www.nhsia.nhs.uk/erdip/pages/evaluation/ docs/polsprotreports/teesfinalc&s.pdf). (Accessed 8 July 2003.)

12 NHS Information Authority (2002) *ERDIP EHR Issues and Lessons Learned Report.* (www.nhsia.nhs.uk/erdip/pages/docs_egif/lessons/LocalandNational EHRImplementationIssues2.15.pdf). (Accessed 8 July 2003.)

13 Thornbury J (2001) *Walsall Natural Community Patient Consent Policy*. NHS Information Authority, paras 4.1 and 4.2. (www.nhsia.nhs.uk/erdip/pages/ demonstrator/wals/walsall_(12).pdf). (Accessed 8 July 2003.)

14 Department of Health (DoH) (2001) *Good Practice in Consent Implementation Guide: consent to examination or treatment*. (www.doh.gov.uk/consent/ implementationguide.pdf). (Accessed 5 June 2003.)

15 British Medical Association (1999) *Confidentiality and Disclosure of Health Information*. BMA, London.

16 Starr P (1999) Privacy and access to information: striking the right balance in healthcare. In: *Massachusetts Health Data Consortium, 4th Annual Meeting*, Boston, MA, 16 April. (www.nchica.org/HIPAAResources/Samples/privacylessons/ P-101%20Massachusetts%20Health%20Data%20Consortium.htm). (Accessed 13 September 2003.)

Chapter 4

Technology – saviour or villain?

Technology has revolutionised the management of personal data. In nearly all industries, the way data is stored, transferred and retrieved has changed with the advent of electronic databases, powerful search engines, remote computer access, email and the internet. Whilst the health sector may not have led the way in this transition, electronic medical records are becoming increasingly common, and are at the heart of the government's planned restructuring of the NHS. This could have major implications for the privacy of patient data.

The current situation

The health service currently makes very poor use of information and communication technology.[1] Although there are examples of successful information technology developments at a local level, particularly in the context of electronic record systems,[1] these have tended to be conducted in a piecemeal fashion with little consideration either of inter-operability or scalability, preventing them being used at a national level.

This failure to embrace the potential of information technology is largely attributable to inadequate IT expenditure within the health sector,* as well as a lack of central leadership in IT planning and acquisition.[1] To address this situation, the government has unveiled a new IT plan for the NHS,[3] which will complement the overall restructuring and improvement of the service. To implement the plan, the IT budget has been increased dramatically.

---

*In addition to an overall lack of health funding directed toward IT, IT budgets are often redeployed to other areas to relieve short-term pressures.[1] There is also the problem that salaries for IT professionals in the NHS are 40% less than elsewhere, causing a chronic shortage of IT skills.[2]

Why do we need technology?

Paper records were an effective method of storing patient information in the days when such records were relatively brief documents primarily required to refresh the memory of patients' own clinicians. As discussed in Chapter 1, however, more people are now involved in the care of each patient, both during a single care episode and over a patient's lifetime (*see* Chapter 1, p. 4). Many of these practitioners will only be involved with patients for a fairly short period, or will perform a specialised role in patients' care, and they are unlikely to be familiar with all aspects of the patient's condition or medical history.[4] It has therefore become increasingly important that practitioners are able to access all relevant information about patients quickly and easily, a task that can be difficult when this is stored on paper.

Paper records tend to be handwritten and non-standard, their quality and structure often depending upon a particular practitioner's own approach and use of abbreviations and terminology. Information is usually recorded by the date of patients' consultations, rather than by the nature or seriousness of the complaint or treatment. This increases the time and effort needed to find relevant information (or to check that no such information exists) and heightens the risk that important details will be overlooked, leading to the repetition of questions, the performance of unnecessary tests, and even medical errors.[5,6] In a 2002 survey of UK patients with chronic health problems or recent hospital experiences, half reported having had to repeat their health story to multiple health professionals as they moved through the care system, and a quarter had experienced their medical record or test results not having reached the doctor's office in time for their appointment.[7] These occurrences are costly and inefficient, and may 'fuel the public's perception of waste in the health system'.[7]

Difficulties can also be caused by the practice of storing paper records at the place where patients were treated or examined, with the resulting possibility that patients will have numerous incomplete records located around the country, many of which they and their current healthcare provider may not be aware. The fragmented nature of health records was identified as one of the factors leading to medical errors that kill thousands of patients in the USA each year.[8]

Many of these problems can be overcome by storing patient information in electronic databases. Modern databases enable enormous amounts of information to be sorted, analysed, searched and transmitted, rapidly and easily. The ability to search across the data allows information to be accessed in a number of different ways, not just according to the date on which it was recorded.

By linking different record systems, all the practitioners caring for a particular patient can, at the same time and at different locations, access the patient's entire record. This will help to provide a better standard of healthcare, and should reduce the number of errors caused by missing information.[9] It will also reduce the time and cost of exchanging information for referrals, laboratory tests and payments, as well as the time spent collecting and searching for information. Consequently, more time can be devoted to the actual provision of care.* The ease with which electronic data can be combined and analysed is also useful for many of the secondary activities for which medical data is required, such as research, health monitoring and audits.[10]

Although there are relatively few published evaluations of the impact of technology, particularly on patient outcomes, the findings that are available tend to be quite positive.[11] For example, electronic medical records have been found to contain fewer errors and result in overall time savings for doctors,[1] while increasing access to healthcare.[7] These benefits, however, are of little value unless the risks to personal privacy that are associated with electronic records are managed properly.

Is technology a privacy problem?

As the title of this chapter suggests, technology can both protect and threaten the privacy of patient data. Electronic databases need not be any less secure than paper records, and are frequently much better,[12] but because they may be accessible remotely, physical security methods alone do not provide sufficient protection. For many people, the potential for a computer hacker to access a database of patient information, without even setting foot in the hospital, and, in an instant, to share that information with millions of people, is far more worrying than the possibility that paper records will be stolen. Significant concern also arises from the ease with which electronic data can be searched for information, transmitted to a potentially limitless audience, and combined with data from different sources.[13]

Although the rationale for these fears is not unreasonable, electronic databases need not pose a major security risk.[14] If security is made a priority, both in the system's technical specification and in the policies and training that underlie its use, the possibility of unauthorised access to patients' data is minimal, and the protection provided is often better than that routinely applied to paper records. This is partly due to the number of privacy-enhancing functions that can be incorporated into an electronic record

---

* According to a 1995 Audit Commission report, 25% of doctors' and nurses' time is spent collecting and using information.[9]

system that cannot be replicated in paper files. Access control mechanisms, for example, can be used to limit the amount of information that different users can view. So, for example, while a patient's physician may be able to access the patient's full medical history, the physician's secretary may only have access to basic contact details. The automatic generation of audit trails also makes it possible to identify irregular access patterns and breaches of access rights. The technology needed to achieve this level of security is readily available and is not particularly costly.[15]

In most cases, the security measures included in a record system aim to minimise the risk of unauthorised access to data, but do not eliminate it entirely.[16] Although absolute security may be possible, the cost and inconvenience of reaching this standard means it will rarely be desirable in a healthcare setting. The security measures adopted must strike a balance between minimising the potential for unauthorised access and preserving a convenient and useable system. Whilst this may sound less than ideal from a privacy perspective, a similar compromise is made with paper records.

The greatest concern in relation to the privacy of electronic records is not the risk of the system's security being breached, but the potential impact of such a breach if it does occur. The speed and ease with which large volumes of data can be searched, combined to reveal new information about a patient or identify a previously anonymous one, and the relative ease with which this information can be disseminated, means that the misuse of an electronic record system can intrude significantly on the privacy of a large number of people.[13] To ensure that patients' privacy is not jeopardised, it is crucial that there are proper security measures to prevent unauthorised access to the system and to monitor the activities of authorised users.

Requirements for a good clinical information system

For an electronic record system to protect patient privacy effectively, it must be developed with security in mind (with privacy and security measures being built into the initial specifications), and supported by appropriate organisational policies.

In the healthcare sector, desirable security features that help protect patient privacy include:[17,18]

- Access control mechanisms that enable different users of the system to be given access to different levels of data. The information available is limited to the actual information needed to perform the user's particular job. Access can be restricted to the records of groups of patients, and even to

specific classes of information within these, and restrictions can also be placed on users' ability to add or edit information they can view.
- The capacity to generate automatically an audit trail that records all attempts to access patient data, whether successful or not. The audit should also maintain a log of any changes made to the record's contents so that previous versions of a record can be 'reconstructed' if needed. This helps to pick up misuses of the system, identify offenders, deter further misuses, and enables amended information to be retrieved if needed.
- An override facility for use in emergencies and other prescribed circumstances, which allows selected users to view patient data to which they would not normally have access. As this right might be prone to abuse, a separate audit trail should be maintained of all override attempts.
- The ability to strip specified personal identifiers from data sets, as a first stage of making information anonymous. Although it is likely that information will need to be checked before being disclosed as anonymous data, performing at least part of the de-identification automatically will save time and help to preserve patients' privacy.
- Security measures to ensure that access controls on information are not circumvented or lost when a record is transmitted from one computer to another, along with methods to protect the integrity of messages in transit. Under a recent agreement between the NHS, the Department of Health, the British Medical Association and the clinical professions, all identifiable patient information must be encrypted before being communicated over any external network.*

The existence of these 'technical' security measures does little to protect patients' privacy if the system is not used in a context and with organisational practices that themselves support privacy.[15] Passwords, access restrictions and audit trails provide no protection if passwords are shared or stuck on monitors, computers are left unattended while they are 'logged-on', or confidential records are viewed on computer screens in public places. Although these practices may, individually, seem fairly trivial, most privacy breaches result from the carelessness or malice of authorised users, rather than from the work of external hackers or those outside the organisation.[14] Developing and enforcing effective policies for using electronic record systems, combined with appropriate staff training on all aspects of privacy and security, are just as important, if not more so, than the security technologies employed in the system itself.

---

*See NHS Policy, on the 'Security – Policies and Guidance' section of the NHS Information Authority website (www.nhsia.nhs.uk/security/pages/cryptographic/guidance/default.asp? om=m7). (Accessed 1 October 2003.)

Public perceptions

As with all healthcare initiatives, implementing electronic medical records across the NHS will be difficult without the support of the public. For most patients, the biggest concern arising from such records is the possible loss of their privacy and confidentiality. As electronic storage remains a mystery, it is a common source of anxiety; a feeling increased by several well-publicised reports of computer system failures.[13] The potential benefits of electronic records are usually only considered to outweigh the risks if appropriate privacy safeguards are in place.[19]

To ensure the success of the government's plan for electronic records, members of the public must be reassured that these records will protect their privacy. To do this, further consultation is needed to ascertain patients' specific concerns and the measures that they think will manage them. The technology and policies that experts regard as appropriate measures to protect privacy may not be what is needed to gain public trust. For example, patients surveyed by the NHS Information Authority did not regard technological security measures as particularly important in the protection of their electronic information.[19] Although this finding may just indicate that further work is required to educate patients of the different ways technology can protect data, it may also suggest that non-technological safeguards, such as the policy guidelines and staff training that underlie the system's use, will be the more important factors that win (or lose) public confidence.

Putting it all in context

The benefits and risks of electronic medical records have dominated much of the current debate about medical record use and privacy. Given that such records do give rise to new privacy issues, this is unavoidable, but it has caused many people to see technology as the crucial factor in the privacy debate, rather than just one of the many issues to consider.

Technology can improve the security of patient information, and can therefore be used to enforce the access and privacy rules developed, but it cannot conduct the more important task of determining what those rules should be.[15]

Summary

- Technology both benefits and threatens patient privacy.
- The NHS currently makes poor use of technology.
- Electronic medical records can improve the accessibility, accuracy and completeness of patient information.
- Electronic medical records need not compromise patient privacy provided that security is made a priority in system design, and there are appropriate policies to ensure the system is used in a privacy-appropriate manner.
- Further work is needed to improve public confidence in the benefits and safety of electronic records.

References

1 Wanless D (2002) *Securing our Future: taking a long-term view.* HM Treasury. (www.hm-treasury.gov.uk/Consultations_and_Legislation/wanless/consult_wanless_final.cfm). (Accessed 25 September 2003.)

2 Benson T (2002) Why general practitioners use computers and hospital doctors do not – Part 1: incentives. *British Medical Journal.* **325**: 1086.

3 Department of Health (DoH) (2002) *Delivering 21st Century IT Support for the NHS – national strategic programme.* (www.doh.gov.uk/ipu/whatnew/deliveringit/nhsitimpplan.pdf). (Accessed 11 September 2003.)

4 (2003) Poor IT placing patients at risk junior doctors warned. *E-Health Insider.* 14 May. (www.e-health-media.com/news/item.cfm?ID=426&searchString=information%20system). (Accessed 18 September 2003.)

5 Roscoe T (undated) *Paper vs Electronic Medical Records.* The Wisdom Centre. (www.shef.ac.uk/uni/projects/wrp/paper.html). (Accessed 30 September 2003.)

6 Schoenberg R and Safran C (2000) Internet based repository of medical resources that retains patient confidentiality. *British Medical Journal.* **321**: 1199.

7 Blendon R, Schoen C, DesRoches C, Osborn R and Zapert K (2003) Common concerns amid diverse systems: health care experiences in five countries. *Health Affairs.* **22**: 106.

8 (2001) US alliance to promote electronic medical records. *E-Health Insider.* 14 December. (www.e-health-media.com/news/item.cfm?ID=72&searchString=privacy). (Accessed 18 September 2003.)

9 NHS Information Authority (1998) *Information for Health:* para 2.71. (www.nhsia.nhs.uk/def/pages/info4health/contents.asp). (Accessed 10 June 2003.)

10 Health Privacy Working Group (1999) *Best Principles for Health Privacy*. Institute for Health Care Research and Policy, Health Privacy Project, Georgetown University. (www.healthprivacy.org/usr_doc/33807.pdf). (Accessed 24 August 2003.)

11 Mitchell E and Sullivan F (2001) A descriptive feast but an evaluative famine: systemic review of published articles on primary care computing during 1980–97. *British Medical Journal*. **322**: 279.

12 American Health Information Management Association (undated) *Confidentiality of Medical Records: a situation analysis and AHIMA's position*. (www.ahima.org/infocenter/current/white_paper.cfm). (Accessed 19 September 2003.)

13 Neame R and Kluge E (1999) Computerisation and health care: some worries behind the promise. *British Medical Journal*. **319**: 1295.

14 Chin T (2001) Security breach: hacker gets medical records. *American Medical News*. 29 January. (www.ama-assn.org/amednews/2001/01/29/tesa0129.htm). (Accessed 15 June 2003.)

15 Committee on Maintaining Privacy and Security in Healthcare Applications of the National Information Infrastructure, National Research Council (1997) *For the Record: protecting electronic health information*. National Academy Press, Washington DC.

16 Mandl K, Szolovits P and Kohane I (2001) Public standards and patients' control: how to keep electronic medical records accessible but private. *British Medical Journal*. **322**: 283.

17 Denley I and Smith S (1999) Privacy in clinical information systems in secondary care. *British Medical Journal*. **318**: 1328.

18 Anderson R (1996) *Security in Clinical Information Systems*. University of Cambridge. (www.ftp.cl.cam.ac.uk/ftp/users/rja14/policy11.pdf). (Accessed 11 March 2003.)

19 NHS Information Authority, The Consumers' Association, Health Which? (2002) *Share with Care – people's views on consent and confidentiality of patient information*. (www.nhsia.nhs.uk/confidentiality/pages/docs/swc.pdf). (Accessed 20 August 2003.)

Chapter 5

Should different medical information be treated differently?

Medical records contain some of the most personal and private information known about individuals, although some parts of medical records are clearly more sensitive than others. Most patients consider a sore throat, for example, to be less private than the discovery of a sexually transmitted disease or a genetic abnormality. For this reason, patients may be willing to allow certain parts of their medical records to be shared quite widely, such as for research and education purposes, but want access to other parts to be strictly controlled. Is it beneficial to adopt a system of this kind, whereby different types of medical information are treated differently?

The current situation

The Data Protection Act 1998 establishes a single regime for controlling the privacy of all types of personal data. The fact that some areas of information will be more sensitive than others is only recognised to a limited extent by granting a slightly higher level of protection to information that is classified as 'sensitive personal data'. Included in this category is any information relating to an individuals' physical or mental health.* By grouping all medical data together in this way and applying the same level of protection, the Act makes no allowance for the fact that different conditions may be more sensitive than others. Data protection legislation in other countries tends to operate on a similar basis.

In most countries, therefore, the main way of recognising the sensitivity of different types of medical information is not general privacy rules but disease-specific legislation that applies special access and disclosure rules

---

* Data Protection Act 1998, Section 2.

to selected classes of health data.[1] In some instances, this is done by imposing greater restrictions on the extent to which identifiable information about patients treated for certain diseases can be disclosed, as is the case for sexually transmitted diseases in the UK.* In addition, or alternatively, certain medical conditions or events may be made the subject of mandatory reporting legislation, which obliges doctors to provide certain information to a specified authority, irrespective of patients' wishes.** In most countries, however, special privacy protections of this kind are applied to only a relatively small number of conditions.† All other medical information is protected by the one set of rules and policies. This is likely to change as more medical records come to be managed electronically.

Electronic records

The introduction of electronic medical records has opened up new opportunities for applying different rights of access to different types of information. Whereas anyone with access to a paper record can potentially view all the information it contains, irrespective of whether it is relevant to their work, electronic records enable different access controls to be applied to each section of the record. This enables restrictions to be imposed on the amount and type of information that is accessible to health professionals, administrative staff and other groups who use patient records, with access being limited to the information required to perform their particular duties.

The least controversial application for this enhanced ability to control access to medical records is limiting the access rights of receptionists, so that they can view and amend contact details and other administrative information, but are not able to see patients' medical data. The technology can, however, also be used to conceal parts of the medical record from health professionals directly involved in patients' care. Depending on the nature of

---

* NHS (Venereal Disease) Regulations 1974 and NHS Trusts (Venereal Diseases) Directions 1991. Identifying information may not be disclosed other than to a medical practitioner in connection with the patient's treatment or to prevent the spread of the disease.
** For example, in the UK pregnancy terminations must be reported (Abortion Act 1967, Section 2 and Abortion Regulations 1991).
† For example, cancer is a notifiable disease in the USA, Canada and some European countries but not in the UK. In many countries, there is also considerable variation between the disclosure requirements of each state. In Australia, for example, only South Australia requires doctors to notify the authorities if a person suffers from a disability that will endanger the public when he or she drives. All other states are silent on the matter, except New South Wales, which encourages, but does not demand, disclosure, by providing legal immunity to doctors who make a report. There are similar variations between the US states.

the information in question, the type of care being provided, or the healthcare provider's particular role in the treatment programme, it may not be necessary for healthcare providers to have access to a patient's entire medical history. A regime of this type, operating in the Netherlands, is considered in Box 5.1.

Box 5.1

X/Mcare case study[2]

Meerkanterm, a large psychiatric hospital in Amsterdam, uses a privacy-enhanced database system for patient records, called X/Mcare. Within the system, medical records are divided into three separate domains of patient information:

- Identity data, such as patients' names, contact details and hospital-assigned patient number, and an encrypted version of the carer-identification number of the psychiatrist in charge of their care (called the 'lead psychiatrist').
- Carer information, being the names and encrypted carer-identification numbers of patients' carers.
- Clinical data, such as patients' symptoms, diagnosis and treatment plan.

By separating patients' records in this way, users of the system can be granted access rights to some, but not all, of a patient's information. The lead psychiatrist is the only person with access to the patient's entire medical record. Administrators can access every patient's record, but are only able to view the identity and carer information, not the clinical data. Researchers, on the other hand, can access the clinical data, but not the first two domains, preventing them from identifying patients.

A facility for emergency access to the entire medical record is available, but this would obviously only need to be used if the lead psychiatrist was not available when an emergency arose. An audit file is created whenever the emergency access is invoked, reducing the likelihood that information will be misused.

Is it a good option?

It is appealing to classify health information according to its sensitivity. Not only does this act as a reminder that certain parts of the medical record are particularly private, but it also enables highly sensitive information to receive the additional protection it requires, without unnecessarily restricting the use that can be made of the remainder of the record.

This type of system also seems to have the support of patients. Research conducted by the NHS Information Authority found that, while most people were comfortable with their general practitioner, hospital doctors and emergency services having access to their medical data, they wanted the ability to limit access to information they felt was particularly sensitive.[3] People were especially concerned about the release of sensitive information to 'single issue' healthcare providers such as chiropodists and dentists. Given this support, and the availability of technology that is capable of controlling access in this way, the case for disease-specific segregation of medical records seems quite strong.

Managing such a system can, however, be difficult from an administrative and risk management perspective.[4] Determining the access rights that should be applied to each piece of data in a medical record will be a time-consuming, and therefore costly, exercise, requiring ongoing attention. A patient may have been admitted with one condition, only for a 'more sensitive' condition to be discovered, or an embarrassing type of treatment or other event may take place, to which access should be restricted. Segregating the information in medical records will also result in different requirements applying to different pieces of information that logically seem to belong together, increasing the risk that relevant data will be overlooked.

The biggest problem with applying different levels of protection to different parts of a medical record lies in determining the classes of information that require additional protection. What constitutes sensitive medical information differs from decade to decade and from one individual to another.[4] An unmarried woman's use of contraception, for example, is likely to be considered less sensitive today than it was 30 years ago. Equally, within any time period there are marked variations between the views of different individuals. Sometimes this variation relates to religious or cultural beliefs, so that a Catholic using contraception may still consider that information to be particularly sensitive, despite the general change in community attitudes. Different views may also arise from differences in individual patients' sensitivities or embarrassment thresholds, or the degree to which they have been open about their medical history with friends and family. A woman who terminated a pregnancy without informing her partner, for example, is likely to attach greater significance to the need to keep that matter confidential, compared with a woman who was open about her decision. Although there are likely to be some clear examples that most people agree are particularly sensitive, in most cases there will be a substantial variation in views. In the NHS Information Authority survey, the majority of respondents regarded pregnancy terminations and information about sexual and mental health as highly sensitive, but felt that each individual would inevitably have additional concerns.[5]

Given these individual differences, patients should ideally be given some control over the types of information that receive additional privacy protection. If, because of the design of the system or the nature of the particular organisation, patients cannot be given complete freedom of choice, they should at least be able to add further items to the organisation's standard list of sensitive information.

Patients are also likely to have different views about who should be entitled to see the sensitive parts of their medical records.[5] A common request would be to deny administrative staff access to sensitive information, which will rarely cause problems, as the hidden data will not usually be relevant to their duties. By contrast, risks may arise if patients request that information be withheld from some or all of the health professionals involved in their treatment, as knowledge of a patient's full medical history is usually considered vital to the provision of safe and effective medical care. Even information that initially does not appear relevant could prove useful in making an accurate diagnosis, or when dealing with complications that arise during a seemingly unrelated procedure or course of treatment. Patients may not appreciate this possibility, particularly where the information concerned does not appear to have a direct and significant bearing on their current care. Alternatively, protecting the privacy of particular information may be so important that, despite their understanding of the potential dangers, patients are willing to accept the risk. Although it has been argued that a certain amount of information is required for doctors to fulfil, or to show they have fulfilled, their professional duties,[6] the principles of autonomy and free choice suggest that, in so far as limiting access to information only places the patient at risk, patients' wishes should be paramount.*

Even where information is important to protect either the health of the patient or the safety of the medical team, it may be possible to provide the necessary protection without disclosing, or with only minimal disclosure, of the sensitive information. For example, a general warning that body fluid precautions need to be followed can protect the safety of those treating an HIV-positive patient, thus avoiding the need to reveal the patient's HIV status. The additional level of privacy resulting from limiting information in this way, however, can be illusory, as it is often possible to deduce what is hidden from that which is disclosed.[1] For example, a patient's pharmaceutical record, which should be available to healthcare providers to avoid

---

* According to the British Medical Association, 'individuals may knowingly compromise their own safety but not that of other people'.[7]

adverse drug reactions, will often reveal the patient's condition, as many drugs, such as Prozac and AZT, are only prescribed for one thing. Equally, patterns of diagnostic tests or clinical attendance could signal the presence of a particular genetic condition. Even where the available information does not definitively indicate what has been hidden, a suspicion, even one that is wrong, can be equally damaging to a patient's pursuit of privacy. Although it is possible to reduce the potential for such inferences to be made, by not highlighting the presence of hidden information, this can also give rise to problems, particularly in emergency situations.[8]

An important question in allowing patients to apply different privacy restrictions to different parts of their medical records is whether, after all the effort and expense of establishing such a system, it will actually be used. Research conducted by the NHS Information Authority indicated that, whilst respondents were generally in favour of having a mechanism for providing extra protection for sensitive information, few would use it.[5] Although this may change when patients become more familiar with what is contained in their medical records, through the ability in the future to access their electronic medical records online, there is no guarantee of this. If the mechanism is not widely used, it is arguably not cost-effective to offer it at all. On the other hand, the mere existence of a right to increase the privacy of particularly sensitive information, whether or not it is exercised, may help ease concerns about the privacy of electronic records, which would itself be beneficial.

The NHS approach

The NHS Information Authority is advocating a patient-controlled approach to protecting highly sensitive health information. It is proposing to include a 'virtual sealed envelope' in the electronic health record system currently being developed,[3] into which patients could elect to place sensitive information. Patients' explicit consent would be required before anyone could access the contents of that envelope. This regime requires there to be some method by which patients can nominate the information they wish to include in the envelope and update that decision over time, as well as a means of recording their responses to specific and general requests for access. Whether this has any significant effect on staff workloads depends to a large extent on the structure of the electronic health record system ultimately adopted, in particular whether adding or removing items from the envelope can be performed by patients themselves and, if so, the relative ease by which this can be done. An intuitive and accessible system will enable more people to perform these tasks personally, although a minority of patients will never be willing or able to do this, irrespective of the design of the system.

Although the NHS Information Authority has not released detailed information about the exact specifications of the virtual sealed envelope, it does anticipate the need for there to be limited exceptions when the envelope can be accessed without consent, such as in emergency situations where consent cannot be obtained. It has also indicated that individuals or organisations not treating the patient may be able to access the envelope in very limited circumstances where 'the law allows it or requires it'.[3] By including accesses that are merely allowed by law, this exception could reduce significantly the extent to which the sealed envelope increases privacy protection.

To date, the NHS Information Authority has not indicated whether the existence or amount of information in the envelope will be flagged in patients' general medical records, nor whether there are any types of information, such as current medication, which cannot be included in it.

Special class of data: genetic information

Genetic data is a particularly sensitive type of medical information. As it reveals details about patients' likely future health, knowing this information could be very beneficial to third parties who have a vested interest in their future, such as health insurers, employers and banks. For this reason, the possibility of affording it special privacy protection has been considered in many jurisdictions.[9]

Genetic data can be distinguished from other types of health information by its ability not only to reveal information about the genetic makeup and health of individual patients, but also their families; its disclosure can affect many people. This raises difficult legal and ethical questions, such as whether a family member is entitled, despite the duty of confidentiality, to be informed of a genetic risk that has been detected in one of their relatives. If a patient is diagnosed with a genetic disease, it is usually advisable to screen other members of their family to determine whether they suffer from the same condition or are carriers. The family, therefore, has a strong interest in this information and could be badly affected if their position is not considered. As with other medical information, however, the discovery of a genetic risk or condition is protected by the duty of confidentiality, so cannot normally be disclosed without patients' consent.

Usually this will not give rise to any problems, as most patients will want their family to be informed of such a finding, but this cannot be presumed. A survey in the USA found that 56% of women felt that written consent should be obtained before a spouse or immediate family member is told about genes that increase susceptibility to breast cancer.[10] Although many of the respondents indicated that, if asked, they probably would consent to the disclosure, there are many reasons why patients may not want to share such a discovery. This could be because of estrangement or family conflict, or to avoid being treated differently or causing worry. If patients are not willing to provide their consent, doctors are faced with a difficult dilemma.

As discussed in Chapter 8, pp 105–6 breaching the duty of confidence is lawful where it is required by public interest, such as to prevent a serious crime, a serious and imminent threat to public health, or a serious and imminent threat to the life or health of another individual. In the USA this situation has been taken a step further, with doctors now considered to be under an actual duty to breach patient confidentiality where there is an imminent risk of serious and preventable harm to an identified other. This duty was first recognised in the case of a psychiatrist who was held to have been under a duty to breach confidentiality when a patient informed him that he intended to kill a particular person.* The risk of a genetic condition or susceptibility, however, is very different from this type of situation, and is unlikely to be considered to give rise to either a public interest that justifies breaching confidentiality or the more specific US duty to act.[11]

Failure to disclose a genetic condition does not cause any direct risk to an identified individual; but it does deprive a group of people of the opportunity to be tested, and potentially benefit from early treatment. Depending upon the condition in question, the risk of others carrying the affected gene may be quite low, and there is always a chance that family members will discover that they have the condition through other means, such as routine examinations. Moreover, if there is no effective cure, and early treatment may not provide any particular advantage, the risk does not relate to a preventable harm. Overriding a patient's decision not to inform their family of the genetic risk, therefore, is unlikely to be justified.

When this dilemma was put to 12 Dutch general practitioners, a very different conclusion was reached, with most deciding that their duty not to harm patients overrode their duty of confidentiality.[12] As a result, if they were unable to convince a patient to inform their relatives of the discovery, they would insist on disclosing the information to any family members who were also their patients, after having informed the original patient of their intention to do so. The problem with this approach, at least under UK law, is that a doctor's duty to one patient is not affected by his or her duty to another.[13]

---

* Tarasoff v Regents of University of California 551 P.2d 334 (Cal Sup Ct 1976).

Of course, respecting confidentiality does not necessarily mean that doctors should do nothing. Doctors can attempt to change a patient's mind by warning of the risks of concealing the diagnosis, discussing the patient's reasons for not wanting to disclose it, and offering to keep the patient's identity secret when informing other family members. Equally, if any of the family members who are also the doctor's patients ever present with symptoms of the condition, the doctor immediately could recommend that they be tested, without disclosing the background knowledge that contributed to this suggestion. It is, however, both illegal and unethical to carry out such a test surreptitiously.*

The British Medical Association (BMA) provides guidelines for dealing with dilemmas of this sort, but by phrasing its advice in fairly general terms leaves much of the decision making to individual health professionals. According to the BMA, whether or not doctors should go against patients' wishes depends upon the severity of the disorder, the reliability of the screening process, the action relatives could take to protect themselves if they were aware of the risk (including reproductive decisions), the harm and benefit resulting from both giving and withholding the information, and patients' reasons for refusing to share it.[7] If, on balance, disclosure is justified, the BMA advises that it should be done in a way that does not identify the patient, after informing the patient of the doctor's intention to take this action. The guidelines also raise the need to approach the issue with the other family members in a sensitive manner that respects their right not to be informed.

Summary

- Some types of medical information are more sensitive than others. The Data Protection Act 1998 treats all medical information the same way, but some people argue that particularly sensitive types of medical data should be subject to tighter privacy rules.
- Advantages of treating different information differently:
  - certain types of medical data have a greater capacity to harm patients if misused
  - most patients appear to want sensitive information to be treated differently
  - it may reduce public concerns about health data privacy.

---

*Sidaway v Board of Governors of the Bethlem Royal Hospital and the Maudsley Hospital (1985) 1 All ER 643.

- Disadvantages of treating different information differently:
  - it may cause administrative difficulties and increase costs
  - limiting the information available to the health professionals involved in treating the patient could harm the patient or others
  - it will not be cost-effective if patients do not use the system.
- Questions to be resolved:
  - who decides what types of medical data should be classified as particularly sensitive (each individual patient or policy makers)?
  - should it be compulsory for certain information to be available to the medical team, even if the patient refuses (e.g. pharmaceutical record)?
- Genetic data: a special category of medical information as it reveals information about patients' current and future health and that of their families.

References

1 Cushman F and Detmer D (1998) Information policy for the US health sector: engineering, political economy and ethics. *Milbank Quarterly Special Edition Electronic Article*, January. (www.milbank.org/art). (Accessed 5 September 2003.)

2 Performance and Innovation Unit (2002) *Privacy and Data Sharing: the way forward for public services*. (www.number-10.gov.uk/su/privacy/index.htm). (Accessed 30 October 2003.)

3 NHS Information Authority (2002) *Caring for Information – model for the future*. (www.nhsia.nhs.uk/confidentiality/pages/consultation/docs/caring_model.pdf). (Accessed 8 July 2003.)

4 Kunitz and Associates Inc (1995) *Final Report of the Task Force on the Privacy of Private Sector Records*. US Department of Health and Human Services. (http://aspe.hhs.gov/pic/pdf/5879.pdf). (Accessed 30 September 2003.)

5 NHS Information Authority, The Consumers' Association, Health Which? (2002) *Share with Care – people's views on consent and confidentiality of patient information*. (www.nhsia.nhs.uk/confidentiality/pages/docs/swc.pdf). (Accessed 20 August 2003.)

6 Markwel D (2001) Commentary: open approaches to electronic patient records. *British Medical Journal*. **322**: 287.

7 British Medical Association (1999) *Confidentiality and Disclosure of Health Information*. BMA, London.

8 Anderson R (1996) *Security in Clinical Information Systems.* University of Cambridge. (www.ftp.cl.cam.ac.uk/ftp/users/rja14/policy11.pdf). (Accessed 11 March 2003.)

9 Crosbie D (2000) *Protection of Genetic Information: an international comparison.* Human Genetics Commission. (www.hgc.gov.uk/business_publications_international_regulations.pdf). (Accessed 4 November 2003.)

10 Benkendorf J, Reutenauer J, Hughs C *et al.* (1997) Patients' attitude about autonomy and confidentiality in genetic testing for breast–ovarian cancer susceptibility. *American Journal of Medical Genetics.* **73**: 296–303.

11 Weijer C (2000) Family duty is more important than rights. Contribution to ethical debate 'Results of genetic testing: when confidentiality conflicts with a duty to warn relatives'. *British Medical Journal.* **321**: 1464.

12 van der Wouden J and van Amerongen H (2000) View from Dutch general practice. Contribution to ethical debate 'Results of genetic testing: when confidentiality conflicts with a duty to warn relatives'. *British Medical Journal.* **321**: 1464.

13 Leung W (2000) Case study. Contribution to ethical debate 'Results of genetic testing: when confidentiality conflicts with a duty to warn relatives'. *British Medical Journal.* **321**: 1464.

Chapter 6

Accessing your own record

Very few patients know the complete contents of their medical record. Although they usually have a fair idea of the type of information it contains, based on what they have told their healthcare provider and the treatment they have received, their knowledge is often vague and incomplete, particularly over time. They are also usually unaware of any additional information that was recorded without their knowledge, such as the doctor's thoughts and impressions and speculative differential diagnoses.

Until recently, this lack of awareness was not seen as a problem. As medical records are created for the primary purpose of assisting health professionals in carrying out their professional duties, many doctors considered it unnecessary, and potentially distressing, for patients to be given access to them. Patients were not encouraged to read their medical records, and those who sought to do so often encountered difficulties. Although this view is slowly changing, patient access to medical records remains relatively uncommon. In part, this results from a belief, shared by both patients and healthcare providers, that interest in accessing one's medical record only arises when patients are dissatisfied with the care they have received and are considering making a complaint. Medical records often provide the best evidence of patients' conditions and the treatment they received, which will help to determine whether patients want to take their grievances further and, if so, the records will form part of their evidence at trial.

Granting patients access to their medical records, however, can also provide the additional benefit of improving the quality of care they receive. Patients who have read their records can engage in more informed and meaningful discussions with their healthcare providers, can validate the accuracy of what has been recorded, and often have a better understanding of their health problems.[1] Equally, reading through the record may remind patients of additional, relevant information that they previously had not thought to disclose. Even for those patients who do not elect to check what has been recorded about them, merely having the right to do so may improve their sense of control over, and involvement in, their healthcare, and reassure them of the professional way in which their information is used and stored. This may help to alleviate their privacy concerns.

Pre-Data Protection Act 1998 access rights

Until the 1980s, there was no statutory requirement for doctors to grant patients access to their medical records. Patients therefore had to rely on the limited rights of access available under the common law. As health records are owned by the relevant healthcare provider, not by patients,* the only basis upon which healthcare providers could be required to comply with a request for access was the doctor's duty to act in a patient's best interest. The obligation to show patients their records or a summary of their contents only arose, therefore, where doing so served patients' best interest.** Where access was not considered to be in a patient's interest, a request could be refused. Given the paternalistic view of medicine prevailing at the time, refusals were not uncommon. Many doctors viewed the sharing of medical records as, at best, unnecessary and, at worst, detrimental to patients' well-being.[2]

Even where access was considered appropriate, the record was usually provided to a healthcare provider nominated by the patient, rather than to the patient directly. According to the Court of Appeal, the common law only requires that patients be given direct access to their medical records in exceptional circumstances, such as where a patient moving overseas has a health condition that makes it likely he or she will require treatment before having an opportunity to nominate a successor doctor.** As a general rule, the common law does not entitle patients to access their records out of sheer curiosity or to gain a better understanding of their medical condition or treatment.

Patients' rights to access their medical records were significantly increased following the introduction of the Data Protection Act 1984 and the Access to Health Records Act 1990, both of which imposed statutory obligations on healthcare providers to disclose health record information to patients. Both Acts, however, were limited in their scope. The 1984 Act applied exclusively to electronic records,[†] whereas the 1990 Act was limited to manual records compiled after November 1991.[‡] For manual records created before that date, access continues to be governed by the common law.

---

* This is because they were created by the doctor for the purpose of carrying out his or her professional responsibilities. Despite being the records' owners, doctors are limited in what they can do with them by the various duties owed to patients, such as the duty of confidentiality and the duty to act in the patient's best interest (R v Mid Glamorgan Family Health Services Authority (1995) 1 All ER 356).
** R v Mid Glamorgan Family Health Services Authority (1995) 1 All ER 356.
[†] Data Protection Act 1984, Section 1.
[‡] Access to Health Records Act 1990, Section 5(1)(b). It was only necessary to give access to information collected before that date where it was necessary to make sense of a record disclosed under the Act.

The Data Protection Act 1998 scheme

The Data Protection Act 1998 introduced a general right for all patients allowing them access to their medical records, irrespective of how the records are stored or when they were created.* This right came into effect on 1 March 2000. Records are obtained under the Act by submitting a written request, containing sufficient information to enable the healthcare provider to identify the patient and locate the requested information, together with the relevant fee.** The healthcare provider must respond to such requests promptly, and in no more than 40 days. A shorter response time may be expected where the requested information is provided systematically for some other purpose.[4]

This statutory right of access is, of course, additional to doctors' discretion to show patients their records voluntarily.[5] Nothing in the legislation stops doctors continuing to respond to informal requests, and in many instances this will continue to be the preferred method of obtaining access. However, where the doctor–patient relationship has broken down (such as amid accusations of misconduct), or the request involves considerable effort or expense on the part of the healthcare provider, it may be necessary for patients to rely on their statutory rights. This is also likely to be the case in big institutions, where the doctor–patient relationship is less personal.

Patients accessing their medical records under the Data Protection Act 1998 are entitled to receive a copy of the record and, importantly in a medical context, have any unintelligible terms explained.† If it is not possible to provide a copy of the record, or if doing so would involve a disproportionate effort, patients may only be entitled to view it. Whether the effort is disproportionate depends on the cost, time and difficulty of providing a copy, and on the size of the healthcare provider's organisation, versus the effect of not supplying the information in a permanent form.[6] Although it is possible to avoid the cost and inconvenience of making copies by handing over the patient's original record, this practice is not recommended, as it can cause problems for patients (if the original record is lost) and for healthcare providers (if the standard of their care is ever queried).[7]

---

* Data Protection Act 1998, Sections 1, 7 and 8.
** Data Protection Act 1998, Section 7(2). At the time of writing, data controllers could charge up to £10 for providing a copy of an electronic record, and £50 for a copy of a record that is manual or partly electronic and partly manual. Only £10 can be charged if a patient views a record without receiving a copy, and access must be provided without charge for completely manual records that have been accessed in the last 40 days.[3]
† Data Protection Act 1998, Section 8(2).

The Data Protection Act 1998 also entitles patients to be informed of the entities to which their medical record has or may be disclosed.* However, the Act provides little guidance on the level of detail required, simply stating that patients have the right to receive a description of the 'recipients or classes of recipients'** with whom the information has been shared. It is somewhat unclear whether this entitles patients to a list of specific names, or just to general descriptions of relevant categories of people or organisations, such as 'health professionals involved in the patient's care' or 'government-funded research bodies'. The appropriate level of detail probably depends upon the amount of information available to the healthcare provider and the ease with which it can be gathered and collated. Arguably, in the case of electronic records, patients may be entitled to a copy of the audit log, which documents precisely who accessed the record at what time. As audit logs are produced automatically by all electronic medical record systems, and are often stored for security and other internal purposes, the effort and expense involved in providing this information in response to specific requests may not be unreasonable. Making this information available to patients would have the dual benefit of alleviating concerns about the privacy of electronic medical records, and encouraging healthcare providers to develop and enforce appropriate access policies.

An important limitation on the Data Protection Act 1998 right of access is that it only enables patients to obtain their own medical records, not those of other patients, although requests can be made on another's behalf if appropriate authority has been granted.[6] Even parents requesting their child's medical record will require that child's consent once he or she is capable of giving it. Children may exercise any rights under the Act, including the right to access their medical record, when they have reached a level of sufficient maturity to understand the nature of that right, which is presumed to have occurred by 12 years of age.[†]

Exceptions

Although wider than the common law, the Data Protection Act 1998 right of access is not absolute. Healthcare providers can refuse patients access to their medical records if the information they contain would cause serious

---

* Data Protection Act 1998, Section 7(b)(iii).
** Data Protection Act 1998, Section 7(1)(b)(iii).
[†] Data Protection Act 1998, Section 66 brings the Scottish laws governing the age at which children are assumed to be competent into line with those operating in England, Wales and Northern Ireland.[6]

harm to the physical or mental health or condition of a patient or another person.* Whilst there is some overlap between this exception and the right under common law to deny access when it is not in the patient's best interest, the Data Protection Act 1998 exception is expected to be interpreted more narrowly. According to the BMA, the circumstances in which access should be denied under the Data Protection Act 1998 are rare, it not being sufficient that the record may upset the patient.[5] More detailed guidelines outlining the specific circumstances in which this exception should be invoked are expected to be available in the future.**

Even where access to the record is likely to cause serious harm, it is not always necessary to refuse the request completely. It will often be possible to satisfy patients' needs through some other method of disclosure.[8] For example, a patient could be given the record after a few days' 'cooling off' period, or access could be provided through an intermediary who can help the patient to understand the information. It may also be useful to discuss potentially upsetting information with a patient before he or she is given access to it. Where certain information continues to pose a risk despite these measures, the patient should usually be able to see the remainder of their record.[5]

Whether or not access to the record will harm the patient or another person must be determined by an appropriate health professional, as it involves the exercise of clinical judgement.* To ensure requests are dealt with on time, a system should be established to enable administrative staff who receive these requests to identify and contact the most relevant professional, quickly and efficiently. This is particularly important in big organisations where there are a large number of clinicians, and less interaction between clinical and administrative staff.

Patients may also be denied access to information in their medical record if its disclosure is prohibited by other legislation. There is no right of access under the Data Protection Act 1998, for example, to records of adoption and information about fertility treatments.[†] On account of the principle of confidentiality, healthcare providers will also be prevented from disclosing to patients any information in their medical record that relates to an identifiable third party.[‡] The fact that the information is in a patient's medical

---

* Data Protection (Subject Access Modification) (Health) Order 2000 (S.I. No. 413), Section 5.
** Research is being carried out by the Central Office for Administration (reported by Marlene Winfield, Head of Patient and Citizen Relations, NHS Information Authority, during discussions with Heidi Tranberg, in London on 31 March 2003).
† The Data Protection (Miscellaneous Subject Access Exemption) Order 2000, as amended.
‡ Data Protection Act 1998, Section 7(4).

record does not alter the duty of confidentiality to that third party. Disclosure is allowed, however, where the identified third party is a health professional who, in his or her professional capacity, contributed to the patient's medical record or was involved in the patient's care.* This is also the case if the third party has agreed to the disclosure,** although the healthcare provider is not obliged to seek this consent.[5] To avoid persistent, unnecessary requests, healthcare providers also need not comply with a request that is similar or identical to one made earlier by the same patient, unless a reasonable time has elapsed.[†]

Healthcare providers are not required to disclose the grounds upon which patients have been denied access to their medical record.[5] They also need not inform a patient if any information has been omitted from the copy of the record provided to them. Although this secrecy may appear to run counter to the principle of transparency underlying the Data Protection Act 1998, openness in these circumstances could defeat the reason for withholding information in the first place. Being informed of the specific reason why access has been refused may itself cause patients substantial damage. Equally, the knowledge that information has been withheld, or the reason for doing so, may enable patients to deduce the nature of the suppressed information.

Amending the record

A further advantage of granting patients access to their medical records is that it enables them to check the accuracy of what has been recorded. The Data Protection Act 1998 supports this practice by granting patients a specific right to request the amendment of any errors they discover.[‡] As research indicates that errors exist in a large proportion of medical records, this could prove to be a very beneficial power, significantly improving the accuracy and completeness of patient files. For example, when the Bury Knowle Health Centre near Oxford granted patients access to their records as part of the Electronic Record Development and Implementation Programme (ERDIP), 70% of patients found at least one mistake or omission in their record.[9] Although many mistakes were relatively trivial, 23% of all

---

* Data Protection Act 1998, Section 7(4)(c).
** Data Protection Act 1998, Section 7(4).
[†] Data Protection Act 1998, Section 8(3).
[‡] Data Protection Act 1998, Section 14.

records contained an error described as 'very important'.[9] The Centre welcomed corrections from patients, believing that 'the more people who are checking the data and validating it, the less room there is for error'.[10]

Most healthcare professionals would agree with this observation and appreciate feedback from patients, at least where straightforward errors or oversights are involved, such as incorrect addresses or dates of birth, or incomplete pharmaceutical records. However, as medical records also contain very subjective information, such as doctors' clinical impressions of patients and speculative differential diagnoses, there are likely to be many situations where patients and healthcare providers disagree over the accuracy or appropriateness of specific entries. Obviously, this will be particularly common when the information in question reflects negatively on patients, such as any suggestion that a patient has mental health problems, violent tendencies or a drug or alcohol dependency. Patients may also object to the inclusion of correct information that they consider no longer relevant to their care, such as a pregnancy termination, earlier mental health problems or personal issues that have since been resolved.

When patients are concerned about certain information in their medical records they usually want it to be deleted. There is considerable opposition in the NHS, however, to deleting anything other than the most basic, administrative errors, as even incorrect information can prove important in the future. For example, although a speculative differential diagnosis may turn out to be incorrect, it can help to explain why a treatment took a certain course, which may be useful if a doctor's performance is ever questioned. Rather than deleting disputed or objectionable information, therefore, it may be better to insert an amendment into the medical record documenting the patient's objection, which appears alongside the disputed data. This overcomes the problem of losing all record of the entry, but it is unlikely to be satisfactory to all patients, as the objectionable information remains available. A more satisfactory option, therefore, may be to archive damaging or disputed information when it is no longer relevant to patients' care. This would ensure that the information could be accessed if it were required for legal reasons, but would not be visible when the medical record is used for treatment or other routine purposes. This type of arrangement could be particularly effective with electronic records, as time-limited information, such as a speculative differential diagnosis, could be entered in such a way that the system automatically prompts the doctor at regular intervals to indicate whether it still applies. If the doctor decides that the information is no longer relevant, it is archived automatically. If necessary, the record can still be reconstituted to its earlier form by consulting the audit trail, which records when information was amended.

Increased patient access to medical records is likely to lead to a rise in the number of complaints about the information they contain. Patients should initially raise such matters with the relevant healthcare provider but, if they are dissatisfied with the response received, they can bring the matter before the courts, which have the power under the Data Protection Act 1998 to order that inaccurate data be corrected, the medical record be supplemented by a true statement of fact and/or that third parties be notified of the corrections.[5] One such application has already been made,* the outcome of which may have a big impact on the number and nature of future complaints. To prevent such claims becoming commonplace, NHS organisations must give careful consideration to the way they respond to patients' objections when they are first received.

Should patients have access to their medical records?

Much of the resistance to giving patients access to their medical records stems from a belief that the information will be misunderstood or will cause patients damage or distress.[2] It is essential that doctors communicate with each other about patients in a way that is truthful, and, as one doctor put it, most patients find it upsetting to read the 'brutal truth'.**

There is little evidence, however, to confirm these fears. In fact, the opposite was found in a London study investigating cancer patients' reactions to enhanced access to their medical records under the Health Records Act 1990. The results showed that, although few patients had taken the opportunity to read their notes, when they did so they found them informative and reassuring, and had increased confidence.[12] The researchers concluded, 'it is causing few problems and may even be improving the quality of the patient–doctor communication and quality of care'.[4] Similar findings emerged from the Bury Knowle Health Centre trial, discussed above, in which patients were given access to their online electronic health records.[13] Most patients who read their medical records had little difficulty

---

* Jessica Lawrence filed a claim against the UCL NHS Trust in the Watford Small Claims Court in December 2002. She claimed that medical records made by the National Hospital for Neurology and Neurosurgery contained errors and damaging comments that made it hard for her to obtain appropriate treatment. The Trust had noted her objections on her medical record, but maintained its policy of not altering records.[11] At the time of writing, a final decision had not been reported.

** Dr Raj Persaud, consultant psychiatrist, interviewed on 'Woman's Hour', BBC Radio 4, 13 December 2002.

understanding the contents and found the experience useful. Approximately half the patients felt that accessing their record was reassuring, with a third being relieved by what they saw. Overall, the researchers concluded that allowing patients to access their medical records was likely to improve the delivery of healthcare by improving communication between doctors and patients, giving patients a greater sense of control over their medical care, and increasing the likelihood that errors and omissions in medical records will be detected. This trial, and a similar one conducted in London, are considered in further detail in Box 6.1 and Box 6.2.

Box 6.1

Oxford case study[9]

The Bury Knowle Health Centre near Oxford has run a number of trials involving the provision of medical records to patients. Following a trial in 1998, in which a sample of patients were allowed to hold their own paper-based records, the Centre obtained funding from the Electronic Record Development and Implementation Programme (ERDIP) to test the viability of giving patients electronic access to their medical records.

Patients involved in the study could either access their record remotely from their home computer or from private computer booths located at the surgery. Security was maintained by a combination of fingerprint biometrics, a password, NHS Number and date of birth. Patients were able to print all or part of their records.

The trial found that:

- 95% of patients found it very easy or fairly easy to navigate through their electronic patient record, despite several of them having little computer experience
- 80% of patients found it useful to have looked at their record, and 74% thought that the advantages of doing so outweighed the disadvantages*
- 70% of patients found errors and omissions in their records, although half of these were trivial

---

*Only 2% of patients indicated that looking at their record was not useful, with the remaining 24% providing no response to this item.

- among the concerns identified by the patients were the security and confidentiality issues relating to electronic access, in particular remote access, and the possibility of receiving new or bad information, such as abnormal test results, via their electronic patient record.

Patients who elected not to access their electronic patient records gave a variety of reasons for their decision, including lack of interest, fear, confidentiality or security concerns, visual impairment and concern that doing so would imply that they lacked confidence in their general practitioners. Fourteen of these patients attended a focus group, during which their concerns were discussed and the system was demonstrated. At the end of the session, 11 of them had changed their minds and were keen to view their records.

Box 6.2

London case study[14]

Dr Brian Fisher, a general practitioner in south London, has been providing his patients with access to their medical records for the past 19 years. Originally, patients were offered their paper records to read whilst waiting for their appointments. When the surgery converted to electronic records, the waiting room was fitted with private computer carousels at which patients could peruse their records in the same way. Unauthorised access is controlled by the use of fingerprint scans and passwords.

The well-being of the patient and others is assured by only giving access to potentially distressing information in the presence of a doctor, and giving no access to third party information. This is done by vetting the information as it is entered in the record. Also, patients are not obliged to look at their records.

The system has been found to:

- break down barriers between medical staff and patients
- improve patients' understanding
- increase patients' overall confidence in their doctor.

The second argument against giving patients access to their medical records is that it will cause doctors to modify what they would normally record about the patient, sacrificing directness and honesty for diplomacy. As the former Privacy Commissioner for Australia explained, the concern is that 'records will become less frank, candid or informative if they can be seen by the subjects'.[15] However, whilst it is likely that greater patient access rights have made doctors more aware of the way in which they are recording information, there is no evidence that doctors are altering their behaviour in any way that is detrimental to patients. A Canadian report on the confidentiality of health information concluded that it is unlikely 'that any responsible and ethical physician would omit from a medical record any information that, in the interests of proper medical care, belongs in it because of the possibility that the patient may ask to inspect it'.* By making record-keepers more accountable for the accuracy and sufficiency of the records they control, the right of access actually may improve the quality of what is recorded.**

A final argument against patients being able to access their own records is that it will lead to an increase in litigation. Denying access on this basis, however, runs contrary to an important aspect of our judicial system: the individual's right to bring legal action against those who have wronged them. Misuse of this right is controlled by processes built into the judicial system,† not by preventing people from accessing the information they need to evaluate the strength of their claim. In any event, whilst greater rights of access may increase litigation in some circumstances, the reverse may also be true. Depriving patients of access to their medical records could be a potential cause of litigation, as patients may be forced to commence legal action to enable them to obtain their record through the compulsory processes of the court, or they may interpret the denial of access to the record as a sign of a cover up.[16] Even without the backdrop of litigation, doctors' reluctance to show patients their medical records could affect patients' trust in them.

Much of the opposition towards granting patients access to their medical records, therefore, is unfounded, and ignores the many benefits that can flow

---

*Report of the Commission of Inquiry into the Confidentiality of Health Information, Toronto, Ontario, 1980 ('The Krever Report'), **2**: 457, quoted in McInerney v MacDonald [1992] 2 SCR 138 at 429.
** Transcript of Evidence by the Health Information Management Association of Australia at page 95. In: *Report of the Senate Community Affairs References Committee: Access to Medical Records*, June 1997, Australia.
† For example, there are processes for dispensing with frivolous claims and those that lack substance or any chance of success at an early stage, without the matter progressing to a full trial. The possibility that the losing party may be ordered to pay the other side's costs may also deter litigants from bringing fruitless lawsuits.

from greater information-sharing. The degree of benefit, however, will depend upon the way in which the information is provided to patients. Patients must be given sufficient time and privacy to digest the contents of their medical records,* and they should have the option of having a support person present. Queries should be encouraged and answered quickly. Particular care must be taken with releasing new information, such as an abnormal result, that could be upsetting. The majority of patients in the Bury Knowle Health Centre trial expressed some concern about this issue, most indicating that they did not want to be able to access such information until it had been given to them directly by a health professional.[13]

Available but not used

As was the case under the common law and earlier legislation, few patients avail themselves of the right provided by the Data Protection Act 1998 to access their medical records.** For some patients this may reflect a lack of interest in healthcare or health record privacy, or a preference that they do not play an active role in ensuring that their health information is protected. For most patients, however, there are likely to be a number of other factors involved.

Most members of the general public have relatively little knowledge of the Data Protection Act 1998 or of their rights under it.[17] Even if they are aware that they can access their medical records, they may be confused about how they go about doing so, particularly when a large organisation is involved, or they may be deterred by the cost. They may also not appreciate how checking what is recorded in their medical records can improve both their privacy and the quality of care they receive. As patient access to medical records goes against the traditional, paternalistic view of healthcare, it is also likely that most doctors are not encouraging their patients to become involved in this way.

The number of patients accessing their medical records is likely to increase as electronic records become more widespread. A major part of the government's plan for electronic records is to give patients the ability to access their records online, at no charge, from the comfort of their own home.[18] To ensure that patients' privacy is not compromised, the security aspects of the system will be very important. It also will be necessary for

---

*For example, where access is provided through computer terminals in the surgery, they should be located away from the main thoroughfare and positioned in such a way that the screen is not visible to other patients.
** The same trend was found in respect of the Access to Health Records Act 1990.[15]

information to be vetted as it is entered in the system, to ensure that patients do not have access to any information that would normally be withheld from them under the Data Protection Act 1998, such as that which identifies third parties.

Provided these issues are addressed, this could be a very useful method of giving patients access to their medical records. Making it easy for patients to look at their medical records will encourage them to do so, thus enabling them to enjoy the benefits that result from greater understanding of their medical care.

Summary

- The Data Protection Act 1998 gives patients a general right of access to their medical records.
- Access can be denied where:
  - the requested information will cause serious harm to the patient or another person, although this will arise only rarely, and often it is possible to avoid the harm by disclosing the information in a different way
  - providing access will infringe a relevant law
  - the requested information relates to an identifiable third party, except a medical practitioner who treated the patient
  - the request is similar or identical to a request made recently by the same patient.
- It is expected that, as more patients come to access their medical records, there will be an increase in the number of complaints made about the information they contain. Objections can be dealt with by:
  - deleting the information, although this could be problematic if the quality of treatment was ever queried
  - inserting an amendment or a notice of the patient's objection in the record, although the disputed information will still be available
  - archiving the information as soon as it is no longer routinely needed.
- There is little evidence that giving patients access to their medical records causes them harm, negatively affects what information is recorded, or increases litigation.
- The Data Protection Act 1998 right of access is not used very often, but this is expected to change once patients are able to access their electronic medical records online.

References

1 Bergen L (1988) Patient access to medical records: a review of the literature. *AMR Journal*. **18**: 102.

2 Cornwall A (1996) *Whose Health Records? Attitudes to consumer access to their health records and the need for law reform*. Public Interest Advocacy Centre, Sydney.

3 Office of the Data Protection Commissioner (2001) *Subject Access and Health Records*. (www.dataprotection.gov.uk/dpr/dpdoc.nsf), under 'Compliance Advice'. (Accessed 30 March 2003.)

4 Office of the Information Commissioner (2000) *FAQs – subject access*. (www.dataprotection.gov.uk/dpr/dpdoc.nsf), under 'Compliance Advice'. (Accessed 30 March 2003.)

5 British Medical Association (2002) *Access to Health Records by Patients*. BMA, London.

6 Information Commissioner (1998) *Data Protection Act 1998: legal guidance*. Version 1. (www.dataprotection.gov.uk/dpr/dpdoc.nsf), under 'Legal Guidance'. (Accessed 30 March 2003.)

7 Department of Health (DoH) (2003) *Guidance for Access to Health Records Requests under the Data Protection Act 1998*. (www.doh.gov.uk/ipu/ahr/dpa1998.pdf). (Accessed 15 June 2003.)

8 Wynia M, Coughlin S, Alpert S *et al.* (2001) Shared expectations for the protection of identifiable health care information. *Journal of General Internal Medicine*. **16**: 100.

9 NHS Information Authority and Oxford Health Authority (2001) *The Development of Patients' Access to Their Online Electronic Patient Record*. (www.nhsia.nhs.uk/erdip/pages/demonstrator/bury/bury_(5).pdf). (Accessed 13 June 2003.)

10 Jain N (2002) The Bury Knowle EHR Project. *Journal of the Torex User Group*. **48**: 26.

11 UK News (2002) Medical records – a review of December 2002 medico-legal news. *Medical Litigation Online*. (www.medneg.com/news/news.cfm?month= December&year=2002). (Accessed 20 October 2003.)

12 Duncan N (1996) On the record. *Australian Medicine*. **7**: 13.

13 Pyper C, Amery J, Watson M, Crook C and Thomas B (2001) Patients' access to their online electronic health records. Paper presented at the Primary Health Care Specialist Group of the British Computing Society Annual Conference, Cambridge, September.

14 NHS Modernisation Agency (undated) *Developing Patient-held Records*. (www.modern.nhs.uk/serviceimprovement/1338/4668/ CHDCReportCover.pdf). (Accessed 13 June 2003.)

15 O'Connor K (1993) Information privacy issues in health care and administration. Paper presented at the Inaugural National Health Informatics Conference, Brisbane, August.

16 Sampford K (1999) *Access to Medical Record, Research Bulletin 6/99*. Queensland Parliamentary Library. (www.parliament.qld.gov.au/Parlib/Publications_pdfs/books/rb0699ks.pdf). (Accessed 13 June 2003.)

17 NHS Information Authority, The Consumers' Association, Health Which? (2002) *Share with Care – people's views on consent and confidentiality of patient information.* (www.nhsia.nhs.uk/confidentiality/pages/docs/swc.pdf). (Accessed 20 August 2003.)

18 NHS Information Authority (1998) *Information for Health.* (www.nhsia.nhs.uk/def/pages/info4health/contents.asp). (Accessed 10 June 2003.)

Chapter 7

Research

Research conducted through the analysis of data contained in medical records (which, for ease of reference, will be called 'medical record research') has made many important contributions to medical knowledge. Unlike other forms of research, however, it has often been conducted with only limited legal and ethical controls, and without patients' knowledge or consent.[1,2] Although there is no evidence that this practice has caused patients any harm, it is not acceptable under the Data Protection Act 1998. Having to comply with the data protection requirements may make it more difficult to obtain the data needed for medical record research, potentially reducing the quality of research that can be conducted.

Research using medical records

Medical records contain a great deal of information about patients' health status, medical history, lifestyle and use of health services. Analysing this data can increase our understanding of health problems and patterns of diseases, can help to identify new health trends and to assess the effectiveness of different treatments and therapies, all of which help to improve the quality of healthcare.[3,4,5] For example, medical record researchers have uncovered links between certain lifestyle factors and medical conditions, such as that between smoking and cancer.* By comparing demographic differences in disease incidence they have also identified sectors of the community that are at particular risk of contracting certain diseases, enabling preventative treatment programmes to be targeted appropriately.[7]

To achieve these outcomes researchers need access to large, unbiased samples of accurate data.[3] Whilst it is possible for researchers to obtain this data themselves by administering questionnaires and surveys, the required information often already exists in medical records. Reusing this information, rather than repeating the entire collection process, offers a number

---

*Other examples are conditions linked to service in the Gulf War and the propensity of leukaemia in people living near nuclear facilities.[6]

of benefits. Most obviously, it reduces the cost and time needed to conduct research. As research projects can involve samples of many thousands of patients,[8] collecting information from scratch could be a sizeable undertaking. Using information in medical records also eliminates the need for further interaction with patients, which reduces the potential for the research to cause inconvenience or distress. The information contained in medical records also may be more accurate than that which researchers could obtain directly from patients, as embarrassment, poor recall or misunderstanding can cause survey participants to provide inaccurate responses. As medical records are compiled for the treatment of real patients, reusing this source of data also may make the research findings more applicable to the real world.[8]

The effect of the Data Protection Act 1998

As previously discussed (*see* Chapter 3, Box 3.1) the first data protection principle of the Data Protection Act 1998 requires healthcare providers to give patients certain information, referred to as 'fair processing information', when collecting personal data.* As part of this process, patients must be informed of the purposes for which the healthcare provider intends to use or disclose the data. According to the second data protection principle, the information may not be used for additional purposes that are incompatible with the purpose for which it was collected, without the patient's consent.

Where data are used or disclosed for research purposes, however, Section 33 of the Act provides a limited exception, exempting healthcare providers and researchers from compliance with some of the data protection principles. The exemption only applies if the research project is not likely to cause patients substantial damage or distress, and the results of the research will not be used to support decisions relating to particular individuals. For the purposes of the second data protection principle, for example, using information for research will not be considered incompatible with the purpose for which it was collected. The utility of this exception, however, is quite limited, particularly as there is some confusion over how it actually operates. According to the Information Commissioner, the exception does not enable researchers to avoid the Data Protection Act 1998 altogether. It merely excuses compliance with certain, specified data protection principles, with the remainder of the Act, including the first data protection principle, applying as usual.

---

* First data protection principle, Data Protection Act 1998, Part I, Schedule I.

Consequently, patients should be informed, before or during their consultations, if their medical records are to be used for research. If a patient was not so informed, or a healthcare provider subsequently decided to use the record for further types of research that would not have been envisaged by the patient at the time of collection of information, patients should be made aware of this. The Section 33 exception, therefore, provides only limited exemption from the normal Data Protection Act 1998 requirements, and will not enable healthcare providers to routinely disclose medical records for research without patients' knowledge or consent.

Many researchers and healthcare providers argue that it will be difficult, if not impossible, to conduct quality medical record research under the Data Protection Act 1998, and problems are already appearing. In what is unlikely to be an isolated incident, members of one research group reported that, after significant delays caused by complex internal discussions, they received different responses from each of the five NHS trusts from whom they had made the same request for data.[9] Although it is possible that the situations in each trust were sufficiently different to warrant different decisions, it is more likely that the variation in responses was caused by the applicable legal requirements being unclear and untested. Until this uncertainty is removed, many Caldicott guardians are likely to engage in extensive and time-consuming consultation before responding to requests for data, and ultimately will err on the side of caution. This could have a negative effect on research and, consequently, on the advancement of medical knowledge.

There is currently much debate about the best way to overcome this problem. The following sections examine three of the options being considered: obtaining patient consent; the use of anonymous information; and relying on public interest.

Consent

Human subjects can only be involved in medical research if they have given informed, voluntary consent.* This requirement recognises the fact that, although medical research provides many benefits to the general community, for individual participants, it can be time-consuming,

---

*World Medical Association, Declaration of Helsinki. Adopted by the 52nd World Medical Association General Assembly, Edinburgh, Scotland, October 2000. Although this was originally believed to apply only to research involving direct human participation, the revision endorsed in October 2000 clarified that references to 'medical research involving human subjects' includes research on identifiable data.

uncomfortable, embarrassing, painful, and can even cause physical or psychological harm. Given these risks, it should always be up to patients to decide whether they wish to be involved in a research project.

This argument works well in respect of clinical trials and other interventionist types of research, where there is a real possibility of harming or inconveniencing participants. In the case of medical record research, however, which only involves the analysis of previously collected information, with no contact between researchers and participants, the need for consent is less persuasive. Despite having been conducted for many years, there are no reports that this type of research has caused patients any harm.[10] In the absence of a real risk against which participants need protection, obtaining consent is a costly and time-consuming requirement that provides little real benefit. This argument is supported by the fact that very few patients object to their records being used in research when they are consulted.[11] Of the 4286 women contacted to take part in the British Women's Heart and Health Study, for example, only 14 refused to allow their records to be accessed.[1]

There are also practical problems with attempting to obtain patient consent for medical record research, as, unlike other types of research, the potential 'subjects' are not present at the time the study is carried out. Consequently, their consent must be obtained at some earlier stage. To minimise cost and delay, this ideally would be done before or during the patient's consultation. At this early stage, however, the healthcare provider usually has little knowledge of the type of research that may be conducted on the record in the future.[3] This makes it difficult to draft a consent form that is both specific enough to provide patients with a good understanding of how their records will be used but also wide enough to incorporate the vast array of research projects that may arise.

Obtaining a specific consent that only covers the types of projects contemplated by the healthcare provider at the relevant time significantly restricts the extent to which medical records can be used for future research without having to initiate further contact with patients. Projects that fall outside the terms of the consent may be considered new uses of the information, about which patients must be informed. Obtaining specific consents of this kind also increases the administrative workload of healthcare providers, as information sheets and consent forms will need to be updated whenever new types of research projects arise. As patients will provide consent at different times, healthcare providers also need to keep records of the different types of research to which each patient agreed.

To avoid these problems, healthcare providers can obtain a very general consent from patients, such as an agreement that their medical records can be used for 'research purposes'. This enables the record to be used for all types of projects that may arise at any time in the future without the need for further contact with patients. It is doubtful, however, whether consent of this kind serves any useful purpose. 'Obtaining unqualified, blanket consent for yet undefined future health research purposes is often empty and meaningless and may sometimes reduce rather than increase privacy protection.[3] Regulating the use of medical records by patient consent is meant to allow patients to control the way in which their information is used, which helps increase their confidence and involvement in their healthcare. This objective is unlikely to be achieved if patients are not given the basic information necessary to make an informed judgement about how their information should be used, such as the nature and aims of research, the type of body conducting it, and the way in which their privacy will be protected. Failure to give patients this information may increase their privacy concerns and may even cause them to withhold consent.* Obtaining consent to research at the time the information is collected, therefore, may not always be an optimal solution.

Equally, however, there are problems with seeking consent from patients after treatment, which will often be the only way valid consent can be obtained. Patients will need to be contacted whenever they were not informed originally of the possibility that their medical records could be used for research (as will be the case with many older records) and, for more recent records, when the consent they provided does not cover the type of project now proposed. This will cause significant problems.

As discussed in Chapter 3, contacting patients individually is both difficult and expensive.[13] This is a particular problem in medical record research, as individual projects often involve large numbers of records, many of which are old and no longer in regular use.[8] Having to contact patients will increase both the cost of the project and the time required to complete it, making it more difficult to obtain funding. As many of the contact details in the records will be out of date, it may be impossible to trace some patients at all. This could result in the loss of a significant number of potential participants, as illustrated by a study in Minnesota, where researchers were unable to reach or obtain responses from one-third of their patient pool.[14] This affects the quantity and completeness of the data available for analysis and, consequently, the quality of research that can be conducted.[14]

Data quality also will be affected by patients refusing to allow their medical records to be used in a research project. Although overall refusal

---

* For example, in a Canadian study, 57% of patients indicated that, before agreeing to their records being used for research, they wanted to be given specific information about the proposed study, such as the study's name and goals, how it would benefit others and the funding source.[12]

rates are generally very low, they are not proportionate across all patient groups, and could therefore have a significant effect on the results obtained.[15] According to a UK survey, people from higher social groups, older adults and men tend to be more willing than other groups for third parties, such as researchers, to access their records.[1] Particular medical conditions may also make patients more or less likely to agree to their records being used in research.* The effect of these discrepancies on the makeup of the final data pool can be seen in the Minnesota study referred to above. Although only 5% of those contacted refused to allow their records to be used, this included a disproportionate number of young women, casting doubt on the validity and generality of their findings.[14] Bias may also be introduced by the possibility that some healthcare providers, such as those with particularly heavy workloads, will elect not to seek their patients' consent in the first place.[17]

A final problem with needing patient consent for medical record research is the possibility that some people will resent being contacted, or find it upsetting, particularly where the medical record contains information relating to an unpleasant or traumatic period of their life or if the patient in question has died.[8] Patients may be upset by such an intrusion even though they do not actually object to their record being used in the particular project.

In many situations, therefore, consent will not be an appropriate basis upon which to conduct medical record research.

Anonymous information

Medical record researchers usually are not interested in the actual identities of those they are studying. Although the data being analysed is obtained from real patients, the research objectives can usually be achieved without access to identifying information. Consequently, it is often possible to use anonymous data. As patients cannot be identified from this data, the research does not threaten patients' privacy. This approach also does away with the need to obtain patients' consent, as anonymous data is not protected by the duty of confidentiality** or the Data Protection Act 1998.† The use of

---

*For example, patients with schizophrenia may be less likely to consent to their medical records being used for research due to the paranoia that is often associated with the condition. This could affect the quality of the patient sample, as the patients agreeing to take part in the study are likely to be less afflicted by schizophrenia than those refusing.[16]
** R v Department of Health, ex parte Source Informatics Ltd (2000) 1 All ER 786.
† The Data Protection Act 1998 regulates the use and disclosure of 'personal data'. Information about an individual is classified as personal data if the individual can be identified from it alone or in conjunction with other data available, or likely to be available, to the data controller (Data Protection Act 1998, Section 1(1)).

anonymous data, therefore, is a practical and cost-effective way of conducting research without invading patients' privacy, and is therefore the preferred approach of the Department of Health.[18] As discussed in Chapter 10, however, it can be difficult, if not impossible, to make some types of research data completely anonymous.

Anonymous and identifiable data are best viewed as opposite ends of a continuous spectrum, rather than as two distinct categories of information.[2] This concept is considered in further detail in Chapter 10, Box 10.2 (p. 144). As more information about patients is added to a data set, the data moves further toward the identifiable end of the spectrum. Although it is rarely necessary to include obvious identifiers, such as names or full addresses, it is often possible to identify a person from combinations of anonymous pieces of information.* Today's large databases and powerful search engines makes this particularly likely.[8]

Making minor changes to the way in which researchers record and analyse patient data can reduce the potential for the identification of patients to occur.[8,13] For example, information can be rounded or truncated, and the searches that can be performed on computerised data can be limited to prevent the display of search results that contain very few 'hits'.** These methods, however, will not always eliminate completely the risk that a patient will be identified. Some types of data, or combinations of data sets, can never be rendered fully anonymous. This raises the difficult issue of assessing when an acceptable level of anonymity has been reached.

Problems also arise where pseudonymous or coded data are required to enable researchers to link information about patients obtained from different sources, or to track patients' conditions over time. Although, with appropriate safeguards, the use of pseudonymous data protects patient privacy in the same way as fully anonymous data, and is encouraged by both the Information Commissioner[21] and the General Medical Council,[22] its legal status is yet to be determined conclusively.[13] As it remains possible to re-identify patients through the code, pseudonymous information potentially falls within the Data Protection Act 1998 definition of personal data. (*See* definition of 'personal data' in footnote on p. 92.) Thus, researchers may invest considerable time in masking the identity of research subjects in this way, only to discover that they are still subject to the data protection requirements.

---

* In the UK, 98% of people can be unambiguously identified from their postcode and date of birth.[19] In the USA it has been shown to take less than a few hours to identify an individual from his or her birth date, sex and zip code.[4]
** For example, a national database of medical records in New Zealand has been designed so that it will not display queries that would return less than six records.[20]

The use of anonymous or pseudonymous data in a research project can also increase the cost and time involved in conducting the research, as it introduces the additional step of removing identifiers. This process can be difficult and time-consuming, particularly where paper records are involved. Even with electronic data, however, where much of the process can be automated, some manual work tends to be required. Given healthcare providers' workloads, it will usually be preferable for this work to be carried out by the researchers or a contracted third party, particularly where the work is voluminous or complex. To disclose identifiable patient records for this purpose, the healthcare provider would either need the consent of the patients, or the approval, in accordance with the regulations made pursuant to the Health and Social Care Act, of both the Secretary of State and a research ethics committee.*

Despite these difficulties, the use of anonymous data is an effective way of preserving privacy in medical record research. For it to become standard practice, however, clearer guidance is needed as to what is required to reach an acceptable level of anonymity, which will ensure the information is beyond the scope of the Data Protection Act 1998. This and other issues relating to the use of anonymous data are further considered in Chapter 10.

Public interest

As discussed in Chapter 8, confidential information can be used or disclosed, without individuals' consent, where doing so is justified by public interest. Provided sufficiently compelling circumstances exist, there is no reason why this principle could not be used to conduct medical record research without consent. According to both the General Medical Council[23] and the Medical Research Council,[6] if it is not possible or practicable to obtain consent, identifiable data can be used for research provided that a research ethics committee considers the likely benefits of the research to outweigh the loss of confidentiality. However, there are a number of problems with relying on public interest in this context.

First, there is little guidance available as to how the public interest exception applies to medical record research. The courts are yet to consider the principle in this context, and guidelines from government and professional bodies tend to be quite vague. For example, the Department of

---

*The Health Services (Control of Patient Information) Regulations 2002, The Schedule, clauses 4 and 5 and paragraph 1.

Health's draft confidentiality code of practice for NHS staff merely provides that the public interest may justify the use of identifiable medical information in research without consent 'in some circumstances' where the project is of 'such significance' or patients cannot be located.[18] It gives no indication of what types of research will be considered more significant than others, or the amount of effort that must be invested in trying to contact patients. It is therefore difficult for research ethics committees to assess public interest claims, which in turn makes it difficult for researchers to predict how an application will be judged.

There is also some doubt as to whether ethics committees are qualified to determine public interest questions in the context of medical record research. Although it seems sensible for the decision to be made by an independent, expert body, rather than the individual researchers, ethics committees are not always well equipped to deal with privacy issues.[8] They are often far more practised at considering the types of issues raised by interventionist research projects, which involve substantial patient interaction. Evidence from the USA suggests that their equivalent of research ethics committees have been less rigorous in their consideration of privacy risks compared with physical and emotional ones.[24] This is exacerbated by uncertainties about the role ethics committees should play in dealing with data protection and confidentiality.[9] Relying on public interest to gain access to medical records for research, therefore, is fraught with uncertainty.

One way of removing some of this uncertainty is enacting special legislation that expressly exempts research from the requirements of the Data Protection Act 1998 in specified 'public interest' type circumstances. To completely solve the problems of conducting research under the Act, this legislation would have to go further than the Section 33 exception, which, as discussed above, only excuses compliance with specific parts of the Act.[25]

The government has gone some way towards doing this by the enactment of the Health and Social Care Act 2001, which gives the Secretary of State the power to make regulations authorising or requiring the processing of identifiable patient information for medical purposes that benefit patient care or are in the public interest.* The regulations created pursuant to this power allow certain types of medical record research to be conducted without consent, such as that investigating cancer and communicable diseases. They also enable researchers to process patient data without consent for the purpose of analysing geographical data, identifying and contacting patients to gain their consent, and making medical records

---

* Health and Social Care Act 2001, Section 60.

anonymous.* Approval is required from the Secretary of State and a research ethics committee.

The government has recently released plans to increase the activities supported by this legislation. The proposed changes will allow approved groups to process patient information held in certain databases for the purpose of managing and planning healthcare services and screening programmes, and assessing and monitoring the performance of healthcare services and service providers.[26] The database containing the information must be approved by the Secretary of State for Health, and the particular processing must be approved by the Secretary of State and the Patient Information Advisory Group (PIAG). These changes are designed to facilitate the continued operation of a number of national databases of patient information that were originally established for finance and management purposes, but now have potential research uses.** At the time of writing, the Department of Health was conducting a public consultation on the proposed changes.

Although the power created by the Health and Social Care Act 2001 may assist medical record researchers in the short term, it has generated a great deal of controversy,[20,27,28,29] which is only expected to increase in light of the proposed changes discussed above. Many people consider it to be an inappropriate power to delegate to the Secretary of State,[8] and are concerned that it could be used too extensively. It is also feared that by enacting this legislation, rather than modernising the UK's record-based research practices, the UK is lagging behind other countries, and risks being excluded from international research networks in the future.[30] The government, however, argues that the power is sufficiently controlled by retaining the need for ethical approval, and requiring the Secretary of State to consult with the Patient Interest Advisory Group and any bodies representing those likely to be affected by the disclosure, before making a decision.[†] In any event, as the Health and Social Care Act 2001 is only intended to provide a temporary power, it does not offer a long-term solution for dealing with medical record research.

---

*The Health Service (Control of Patient Information) Regulations 2002. When processing information under these Regulations, identifying information should be removed as far as practicable.
** Specifically, the NHS Wide Clearing Service (NWCS), the Hospital Episode Statistics (HES) database, the National Health Authority Information System (NHAIS) and the Patient Episode Database for Wales (PEDW).
† Explanatory Notes to the Health and Social Care Act 2001, paragraphs 292 and 293.

Disease-monitoring bodies

The disclosure of patient information to disease-monitoring bodies, such as cancer registries, raises many of the same issues as the use of such information in general medical research. Like medical research, collecting and analysing data about the diagnosis and progression of different diseases has led to important social and medical developments.[17] It has assisted in the development of treatment and prevention programmes, and in the evaluation of existing health initiatives and campaigns. It has also provided valuable information to assist in the allocation of health resources.

Traditionally, patient data have been disclosed to disease-monitoring bodies in an identifiable form, often without patients' knowledge or consent. Aside from a handful of conditions, such as infectious diseases, which are required by law to be reported, most of these disclosures are voluntary, relying on the good will and co-operation of healthcare providers.[17] As with medical record research, the Data Protection Act 1998 severely jeopardises the continuation of this practice. To comply with the Act, healthcare providers need to either obtain patients' consent before disclosing information to disease-monitoring bodies, or should release the information in an anonymous form.

Whilst the GMC favours the consent approach,[22] many healthcare providers argue that obtaining consent for this purpose is impractical, cumbersome, and, in some circumstances, inappropriate[31] and unworkable.* To avoid these problems some data repositories, with apparent success, have amended their information collection practices so as to enable them to receive anonymous information.** A number of other monitoring bodies, including cancer registries, argue that their current administrative and computer systems prevent information being received and managed in an entirely anonymous form (although in most cases the bulk of the identifying data is removed at an early stage).†

---

* For example, in Hamburg, Germany, a ban on the disclosure of patient data to the cancer register without consent led to a 70% drop in notifications, destroying the register's comparative value;[17] in the UK, a belief that patient consent was needed to include patient data in a diabetes register was said to contribute to the register receiving information about only 60% of eligible diabetic patients. This was mainly the result of doctors electing not to seek consent.[32]

** For example, the Yellow Cards through which adverse drug reactions are reported have now been amended to require only the patient's initials and age, rather than their name and date of birth. The healthcare provider should also include some type of local identification number (such as the patient's hospital reference number) to enable follow-up information to be obtained if necessary.[33]

† For example, 85% of the data going into the Communicable Disease Surveillance Centre is unnamed, and the names on the remainder are removed after a period.[34]

The regulations made under the Health and Social Care Act 2001, discussed above, provide some solution to this problem, as they authorise the disclosure of patient-identifying information for the purpose of monitoring the incidence of cancer and communicable diseases.* As these regulations are temporary and only cover two types of medical conditions, however, they do not solve the entire problem. In the long term, consent, anonymity or a more permanent legislative regime will be required.

What is the best way forward?

Medical record research has made significant contributions to healthcare without appearing to have caused any damage (*see* Box 7.1). 'The legitimate sharing of confidential information between healthcare providers and researchers has gone on for many years, providing benefits to individuals and the community. There is no evidence of any harm ever having been caused by this exchange of information whereas restricting data exchange for public health research and practice has the potential to cause damage to public health'.** [1] As the current practice is working, many researchers ask, 'Why destroy it?'[10]

The answer, for good or bad, is that the current method of conducting medical record research cannot continue under the Data Protection Act 1998. Although the Health and Social Care Act 2001 can be used to allow specific types of research to be carried out without patients' consent, it is only intended to be a temporary power. In the long term, the best way forward is likely to be a combination of a number of the alternatives discussed in this chapter.

---

*The Health Service (Control of Patient Information) Regulations 2002, Sections 2 and 3.
**Professor Sir Richard Peto, Director of the Clinical Trial Service and Epidemiological Studies Unit in Oxford, interviewed on Newsnight, BBC2, 18 May 2001 and the Today Programme, Radio 4, 19 May 2003.

Box 7.1

The importance of medical record research

Medical record research has increased medical knowledge and improved the delivery of health services. The following list outlines some of the areas that have been investigated through the analysis of medical records.

- Identifying patterns of health, disease and disability. For example:
  - comparing the health status of different geographic and socio-economic groups
  - tracking the effect of premature birth on later health.
- Identifying the causes of diseases and their effects. For example:
  - investigating the health effects of past exposure to certain substances, such as asbestos
  - examining the incidence of cancer in women who have had breast implants.
- Reducing public health threats. For example:
  - identifying the causes of disease outbreaks
  - monitoring the spread of HIV or AIDS.
- Understanding the utilisation of healthcare. For example:
  - investigating seasonal changes in patient numbers in hospitals
  - identifying demographic variables that affect the decision to seek healthcare.
- Evaluating and improving preventative and therapeutic practices, and programmes. For example:
  - examining the predictive value of screening tests, such as pap smears and mammographic screening
  - monitoring the organisation and quality of cancer treatment
  - identifying the benefits of aspirin and other drugs to people at risk of heart disease.
- Analysing economic aspects of healthcare, such as:
  - the cost of illness and care
  - the cost-effectiveness of different interventions
  - the component costs of different aspects of the healthcare system.

Wherever possible, researchers should obtain specific consent from patients before using their medical records for research, or only use anonymous or pseudonymous data. Where this is not practicable, the research should only proceed if a properly trained and informed ethics review committee decides that doing so is justified by public interest. Such bodies should be given clear guidance on how to make this determination, which, among other things, should take into account the fact that medical record research poses little risk to patients.

Researchers must also ensure that the protection of privacy is given sufficient consideration at all stages of their project. Patient privacy is affected just as much by the way patient information is stored and destroyed, and how research results are published, as it is by the disclosure of the records in the first place.

Summary

- The analysis of medical records has made important contributions to medical knowledge.
- Patients' records are often used in medical record research in breach of the Data Protection Act 1998. Conducting research in accordance with the Act, however, is difficult.
- There are three main options to deal with the restrictions of the Data Protection Act 1998, none of which provides a perfect solution:
    - *consent* – this can be difficult and expensive to obtain, and may reduce both the quantity and quality of data available for analysis
    - *use of anonymous data* – this protects patients and avoids the need to comply with the Data Protection Act 1998, but it is not always possible to make data fully anonymous, and the legal status of pseudonymous data is unclear
    - *relying on the public interest exception* – this could enable medical record research to be conducted without consent, but there is little guidance on how to apply it in this context. Legislation can reduce the uncertainty, but can also be controversial.
- The best way forward for medical record research is likely to be a combination of the different approaches.
- Using medical records for disease-monitoring purposes raises many of the same issues.

References

1 Lawlor D and Stone T (2001) Public health and data protection: an inevitable collision or potential for a meeting of minds? *International Journal of Epidemiology.* **30**: 1221.

2 Goldman J and Choy A (2002) *Privacy and Confidentiality in Health Research.* The Online Ethics Center for Engineering and Science, Case Western Reserve University. (http://onlineethics.org/reseth/nbac/hgoldman.html#f3). (Accessed 30 May 2003.)

3 Canadian Institutes of Health Research (2001) *Case Studies Involving Secondary Use of Personal Information in Research (Draft).* (www.cihr-irsc.gc.ca/publications/ethics/privacy/case_studies_e.pdf). (Accessed 30 March 2003.)

4 Institute of Medicine (2000) *Protecting Data Privacy in Health Services Research.* National Academy Press, Washington DC.

5 Al-Shahi R and Warlow C (2000) Using patient-identifiable data for observational research and audit. *British Medical Journal.* **321**: 1031.

6 Medical Research Council (2000) *Personal Information in Medical Research.* (Updated January 2003.) (www.mrc.ac.uk/pdf-pimr.pdf).

7 Cassell J and Young A (2002) Why we should not seek individual consent for participation in health services research. *Journal of Medical Ethics.* **28**: 313.

8 Lowrance W (2002) *Learning from Experience – privacy and the secondary use of data in health research.* The Nuffield Trust, London.

9 Strobl J, Cave E and Walley T (2000) Data protection legislation: interpretation and barriers to research. *British Medical Journal.* **321**: 890.

10 Doll R and Peto R (2001) Rights involve responsibilities for patients, letter to the editor. *British Medical Journal.* **322**: 730.

11 Tondel M and Axelon O (1999) Concerns about privacy in research may be exaggerated. *British Medical Journal.* **319**: 706.

12 Willison D, Keshavjee K, Nair K, Goldsmith C and Holbrook A (2003) Patients' consent preferences for research uses of information in electronic medical records: interview and survey data. *British Medical Journal.* **326**: 373.

13 Cambridge Health Informatics Limited (2001) *Gaining Patient Consent to Disclosure.* (www.doh.gov.uk/ipu/confiden/gpcd/exec/gpcdexec.pdf). (Accessed 13 March 2003.)

14 Detmer D (2000) Your privacy or your health – will medical privacy legislation stop quality health care? *International Journal for Quality in Health Care.* **12**: 1.

15 Woolf S, Rothemich S, Johnson R and Marsland D (2000) Selection bias from requiring patients to give consent to examine data for health services research. *Arch Fam Pract.* **9**: 1111.

16 Roberts L and Wilson S (2002) Argument for consent may invalidate research and stigmatise certain patient groups, letter to the editor. *British Medical Journal.* **322**: 858.

17 Verity C and Nicoll A (2002) Consent, confidentiality, and the threat to public health surveillance. *British Medical Journal.* **234**: 1210.

18 Department of Health (DoH) (2002) *Confidentiality: a code of practice for NHS staff (draft).* (www.nhsia.nhs.uk/confidentiality/pages/consultation/docs/code_prac.pdf). (Accessed 24 June 2003.)

19 Anderson R (1998) *Information Technology in Medical Practice: safety and privacy lessons from the United Kingdom.* University of Cambridge, Cambridge. (www.cl.cam.ac.uk/users/rja14/austmedjour/austmedjour.html). (Accessed 6 May 2003.)

20 Davies S (2001) *Taking Liberties in Confidence: a report for the Nuffield Trust on the implications of Section 67 of the Health and Social Care Bill.* (http://is.lse.ac.uk/privacy/healthconfidentiality.doc). (Accessed 23 June 2003.)

21 Information Commissioner (2002) *Use and Disclosure of Health Data.* (www.dataprotection.gov.uk/dpr/dpdoc.nsf), under 'Compliance Advice'. (Accessed 10 May 2003.)

22 General Medical Council (2000) *Confidentiality: protecting and providing information.* GMC, London.

23 General Medical Council (2002) *Research: the role and responsibility of doctors.* GMC, London.

24 Lowrence W (1997) *Privacy and Health Research (A Report to the US Secretary of Health and Human Services),* May. (http://aspe.hhs.gov/datacncl/PHR.htm). (Accessed 16 June 2003.)

25 Information Commissioner (1998) *Data Protection Act 1998: legal guidance.* Version 1. (www.dataprotection.gov.uk/dpr/dpdoc.nsf), under 'Legal Guidance'. (Accessed 30 March 2003.)

26 Department of Health (DoH) (undated) *Proposal to Revise Regulations made under Section 60 of the Health and Social Care Act 2001.* (www.doh.gov.uk/ipu/act/nhs_databases_consultation_paper.pdf). (Accessed 10 November 2003.)

27 Anderson R (2001) Undermining data privacy in health information. *British Medical Journal.* **322**: 442.

28 McCarthy K (2001) Health industry warns of 'sinister' government legislation. *The Register,* 13 March. (www.theregister.co.uk/content/7/17567.html). (Accessed 6 May 2003.)

29 Dyer C (2001) Bill gives government power to breach patient confidentiality. *British Medical Journal.* **322**: 256.

30 Anderson R, Hanka R and Hassey A (2001) *Clause 67, Medical Research and Privacy: the options for the NHS.* (www.cl.cam.ac.uk/ftp/users/rja14/hcbillc67.pdf). (Accessed 25 June 2003.)

31 Paterson I (2001) Consent to cancer registration – an unnecessary burden. *British Medical Journal*. **322**: 1130.

32 Burnett S, Woof C and Yudkin J (1992) Developing a district diabetic register. *British Medical Journal*. **305**: 627.

33 Medicines and Healthcare Products Regulatory Agency (2002) *The Yellow Card Scheme: protecting patient confidentiality*. (www.mca.gov.uk).
(Accessed 21 October 2003.)

34 Brown P (2002) Health bodies defend their right to access patient data. *British Medical Journal*. **324**: 1236.

Chapter 8

Public interest

Regulating the use and disclosure of medical records involves balancing the needs and interests of the public with those of individuals. Although modern society places a lot of value on individual rights, the needs of society must sometimes prevail. Parliament has identified a number of situations where this should occur, and has made these the subject of mandatory reporting legislation. It is not possible, however, to identify in advance every situation where disclosure will be required, as the best course of action will often depend upon the specific circumstances in question and the political, social and legal climate existing at the time. In the absence of a statutory obligation to disclose patient information, the duty of confidentiality can be overridden only where doing so is justified by the public interest.

What is the public interest?

It is lawful, and hence not in breach of the Data Protection Act 1998, for a healthcare provider to disclose confidential patient information, without a patient's consent, where it is necessary to protect the public interest.[1] Although neither parliament nor the courts have defined 'public interest' specifically, they have identified a number of factors that should be considered when applying the exception. In deciding whether to disclose confidential information, healthcare providers should weigh the possible harm disclosure will cause to both individuals and the overall trust between doctors and patients, against the benefits that are expected to arise from making the disclosure.[1] This involves a consideration of the nature of the information in question, the level of disclosure required, the intended recipients of the information, the urgency of making the disclosure, and whether there is any way to achieve the public interest without breaching confidentiality.* A disclosure justified by this exception must really be in the

*R v A Local Authority in the Midlands & a Police Authority in the Midlands, ex parte LM (2002) UKHRR 143.[2,3]

public interest, not just 'of interest' to the public;[4] a distinction that has proved crucial in many complaints by celebrities against the publication of their private details by the tabloid press.*

In the medical context, public interest is most commonly used to justify disclosures that are essential to prevent or lessen a serious and imminent threat to public health or the life or health of another individual.[2] The key factor in these disclosures is that the threat is particularly severe. Disclosing information to the police or other authorities to tackle a serious crime, for example, would only be justified if the nature of the crime was very grave, and failure to disclose the information would prejudice its prevention, detection or prosecution to a serious extent. Generally, threats to people are considered more significant than those to property or financial interests, but this is not always the case.[2] For example, although property theft usually would not be considered a sufficient reason for breaching confidentiality, disclosure may be justified where the theft involves substantial amounts of NHS property, as this may cause serious damage to those awaiting treatment.

These examples only illustrate, rather than define, the circumstances in which the public interest exception may arise. It is not possible to provide more detailed guidance, or an exhaustive list of circumstances where the public interest will be a reliable defence to breaching confidentiality, as each case ultimately must be determined on its own merits.[2,4] For the same reason, it cannot be assumed that, just because a disclosure was considered justified in one instance, the same result will be found in similar situations.

Is the public interest exception too uncertain?

Not prescribing the specific circumstances in which the public interest will justify the disclosure of confidential information ensures that the exception remains a flexible concept that is able to adapt to new circumstances, medical developments and changing social conditions. Theoretically, there is no limit to the range of situations where the public interest exception could come into play.

---

* For example, the *Daily Mirror* newspaper defended its decision to publish details of Naomi Campbell's treatment at a drugs clinic on the basis of the public interest. The Court of Appeal, overturning a High Court judgement in favour of Campbell, held that since Campbell had denied being a drug addict, the publication was in the public interest as it exposed her lies. The court held that if an individual gives a public perception that is untrue, it is justifiable for the press to reveal confidential details to expose the lies. In February 2003, Campbell won the right to appeal this decision to the House of Lords. At the time of writing no date had been set for the hearing.[5,6]

With this flexibility, however, comes uncertainty. Although guidelines are available to help healthcare providers to weigh up the various interests, they cannot provide definite answers.*[7] Even where well-established public interest considerations are involved, such as suspicions of child abuse, it is not always easy to identify the right course of action, as no two cases are ever identical. There always will be differences in the likelihood and gravity of harm, doctors' certainty that the risk exists, the extent to which the disclosure of the information will reduce the risk, and the likelihood that patients can be convinced to disclose the information voluntarily or that the risk can be otherwise averted without breaching the duty of confidentiality.

This uncertainty is particularly high for healthcare providers, as very little of the case law dealing with the public interest relates to healthcare settings.** Not surprisingly, therefore, the public interest exception is understood poorly within the NHS. According to the Department of Health, it is incorrectly used to justify some disclosures of patient information, yet not raised in other situations where arguably confidentiality should be broken.[8]

Deciding whether or not to disclose confidential information on the basis of public interest is a matter of judgement for individual doctors. The important factor, according to ethical guidelines, is that doctors are able to justify their decisions.[2,3] Even where the disclosure is made in response to a request from the police or another body, the doctor, as the one who owes the relevant duty, should not release the information unless he or she is satisfied personally of the legality of doing so. Ultimately, however, despite doctors' belief in the validity of their decisions, it is the court that determines whether the disclosure was legal. Whilst legal proceedings can be instigated to determine the correct course of action before a disclosure is made, it is not possible or practicable to go through this process every time patient information is to be disclosed. Relying on the public interest to justify breaching confidentiality, therefore, usually involves a degree of risk and judgement.

How can the uncertainty be reduced?

Reducing the uncertainty in this area would assist healthcare providers to make these difficult judgements and help patients to understand the limits of confidentiality. It is quite difficult, however, to find a workable way of doing

---

*For example, the GMC guidelines provide that 'ultimately, the "public interest" can be determined only by the courts'.[1]
** Explanatory Notes to the Health and Social Care Act 2001, paragraph 295.

this. One solution would be to enact legislation that specifies exactly what is required for a disclosure to be justified by public interest. For this to improve upon the present guidelines, it would need to be very specific, offering something more concrete than another set of factors to consider. For example, the legislation could set out an exhaustive list of situations where disclosure is permitted or required. This would have the unfortunate side effect of significantly reducing the extent to which the public interest exception could be applied to novel situations.

To avoid this loss of flexibility, a possible alternative to this approach is to rely on a mixture of legislation and common law. Under this type of system, mandatory reporting legislation is applied to the most common types of public interest situations (thus increasing certainty), while the common law public interest exception is retained to ensure there is still substantial flexibility. The mandatory reporting legislation should specify the conditions that need to be satisfied to justify disclosure in each case and the channel through which the disclosure should be made. A healthcare provider disclosing information in accordance with such legislation is exempt from any possible legal liability. As healthcare providers will only have to grapple with the existing dilemmas of the public interest exception in new or unusual situations, this system increases certainty and reduces the potential for legal liability without destroying the current flexibility.

The problem with this approach is the disagreement and controversy that inevitably arises when trying to establish new mandatory reporting obligations. Compared with many other countries, the UK has relatively little mandatory reporting legislation.* Many disclosures required for health monitoring purposes, for example, have relied upon doctors' good will, rather than legal obligations; a system that has worked well in the past, but is somewhat threatened by the Data Protection Act 1998 (*see* Chapter 7, p. 97).** In many other situations where information is disclosed for public interest reasons, such as suspicions of child abuse,[1] healthcare providers only have the advice of non-binding guidelines upon which to rely, rather than actual legislation. As a consequence, doctors frequently must rely on their own judgement as to the correct course of action.

---

* For example, notifiable communicable diseases must be reported under the Public Health (Control of Disease) Act 1984 and the Public Health (Infectious Diseases) Regulations 1988. Unlike many other jurisdictions, the UK does not have mandatory reporting legislation covering child abuse, gunshot wounds and cancer.
** In June 2002, the General Medical Council issued new guidance stating that doctors should not, in light of the Data Protection Act 1998, transfer patients' details to cancer registries without their consent.[9] This problem has been solved in the short term by the Health Service (Control of Patient Information) Regulations 2002, made under the Health and Social Care Act 2000, Section 60, which authorises the disclosure of patient data to cancer registries without consent.

Although there are advantages of enacting more mandatory reporting legislation, attempts to do so inevitably give rise to substantial disagreement over what situations should (and should not) be included, and what conditions need to be satisfied to require disclosure in each case. For example, in the UK there is strong opposition against requiring doctors to notify the police or other specified law enforcement authorities whenever patients are treated for gunshot wounds and violent crimes, despite similar obligations existing in other jurisdictions.[10] Despite the importance of reducing firearm crimes and violence, it is feared that an obligation of this kind would place doctors at risk and bring into question hospitals' independence from the police.[11]

An alternative, and less controversial, way of reducing the uncertainty of the public interest exception is ensuring that healthcare providers, when faced with public interest dilemmas, can quickly and easily obtain guidance from dedicated advisory groups or help lines. By providing advice about real situations as and when they arise, these services can give more specific, and therefore more helpful, guidance than that offered in general information booklets. Although there are already a number of organisations providing services of this kind, limited time and information often means that only relatively general advice can be given. To be useful, doctors obviously must be made aware of, and encouraged to use, these services. As the British Medical Association (BMA) suggests, it also may be helpful for doctors to discuss difficult cases with colleagues, provided this can be done without identifying the patient.[2]

Is the public interest exception becoming too broad?

There has been a steady increase in the range of situations in which the public interest exception has been applied successfully, and given its dynamic nature, new applications will continue to arise. There are, however, a number of restrictions, particularly in the medical context, preventing the exception becoming too broad.

The greatest of these limitations is the fact that the public interest exception can be relied upon only in exceptional cases.[1,2] A disclosure to protect an individual, for example, is justified only in 'compelling circumstances', where it is required to avoid a 'substantial risk of harm'.* It is for this reason that the defence is usually limited to the most serious crimes against the

---

*W v Egdell (1990) Ch 359.

person, rather than crimes against property. The disclosure also must be likely to help reduce or avoid that risk, and there must be no other practicable means by which this can be done.[2] Before breaching confidentiality, therefore, healthcare providers should, if appropriate, try to persuade patients to disclose the relevant information voluntarily.

A further restriction on the scope of the public interest exception is that it only provides a narrow exemption from the duty of confidentiality, rather than dispensing with it altogether. Information can be disclosed only to an extent, and in a way, that is appropriate, having regard to the particular interest or potential harm in question.[2] Consequently, it will not always be necessary or acceptable to hand over a patient's entire medical record. In the case of a serious crime, for example, only information strictly relevant to the specific investigation should be released. It would not be appropriate to comply with a general request, such as for information relating to several patients in order to identify potential suspects, unless the factors supporting disclosure were particularly compelling.

The exception is also limited by restrictions on the way in which information may be disclosed. First, it can be disclosed only to those with a 'legitimate interest' in the information,* which is usually the agency or department appointed to deal with the particular risk. It would be very rare in a medical context for the public interest to justify the disclosure of patient information to the media. Second, before disclosing information, it may be necessary to ensure there are appropriate safeguards in place to minimise the extent to which patients' privacy is compromised. For example, in a recent application by a health authority seeking access to medical information to investigate suspicions of misconduct, the court accepted that there was a compelling public interest involved, but was prepared to order the disclosure only if the applicant gave confidentiality undertakings and agreed to keep any public disclosure to a minimum.** In the case of a police investigation, it may be reasonable to obtain undertakings that the information will not be used or passed on for any purpose other than the present investigation.

Despite its flexibility, therefore, the public interest exception is subject to a number of limitations. It is an exceptional defence to a breach of confidentiality, not a back door method for routine disclosures. Of much more concern for most people is the power, under Section 60 of the Health and Social Care Act 2001, to allow identifiable patient information to be disclosed for medical purposes without consent where the Secretary of State, in consultation with advisory bodies, deems it to be in the public interest or the interest of improving patient care. Despite the government's assurances

---

* W v Egdell (1990) Ch 359.
** A Health Authority v X and Others (2002) 2 All ER 780.

that this is a temporary power to be used in only limited circumstances,* the power has received considerable criticism, and there is much concern that it will be used too extensively (*see* Chapter 7). These concerns are likely to rise following the government's announcement that it intends to increase the range of activities covered by the legislation.** At the time of writing, the Department of Health had not concluded its public consultation on the proposed changes, though if reactions to the original legislation are any indicator, much of the feedback will be far from supportive.

Given this controversy, the public interest exception is likely to remain an important basis upon which disclosures of confidential information without consent are made. Although the exception is inherently vague, and therefore a source of uncertainty and confusion for both healthcare providers and patients, this allows it to be applied to novel situations as they arise. To ensure the exception is not used inappropriately, however, those dealing with public interest dilemmas must have access to useful and timely advice.

Box 8.1 gives examples of disclosures that may be justified by the public interest.

Box 8.1

Examples of disclosures in the public interest

The following list outlines a number of situations where the public interest may justify a healthcare provider disclosing confidential patient information. As cases involving public interest must each be determined on their own merit, these scenarios are provided for illustrative purposes only.

- The disclosure of a patient's HIV status to his or her sexual partner, where the patient has not informed him or her and cannot be persuaded to do so.[13]
- The disclosure to the relevant authorities of suspected abuse or neglect of a patient who does not have the capacity to consent, such as a young child or someone with a mental disability, where making the disclosure is considered to be in the patient's best interest.[1] If patients have the capacity to consent, their decision usually should be respected, though the healthcare provider may

---

* Explanatory Notes to the Health and Social Care Act 2001, paragraph 295.
** The proposed changes would enable approved groups to process patient data in certain national databases without consent for the purpose of managing healthcare services and screening programmes, and monitoring the performance of health services and service providers. The changes are designed to facilitate the continued operation of a number of national databases of patient information that were originally established for financial and management purposes but now have potential research uses.[12]

encourage them to disclose the abuse voluntarily. The situation may be different where the abuse is placing others at risk, such as the children of an abused wife.[4]

- The disclosure to the relevant employer or regulatory body that a medical colleague, who is also a patient, has a medical condition, which may place patients at risk.[1,13]
- Disclosure to the medical advisor of the Driver and Vehicle Licensing Agency where a patient is continuing to drive, against medical advice, when he or she is unfit to do so.[1]
- The disclosure to the police of information necessary to prevent, detect, investigate or punish a serious offence, such as murder, manslaughter, rape, treason or kidnapping. Less serious crimes, such as minor thefts, are unlikely to be considered to be of sufficient severity to warrant disclosure. For the disclosure to be justified, the prevention or detection of the crime must be seriously prejudiced without the information, and the information must not be available from another source. If the crime has already been committed and the individual is unlikely to re-offend (as is the case with a mercy killing), it still may be appropriate to disclose the information in some circumstances.[4]
- The disclosure of information about a patient in order to identify the source of an infection or other possible carriers, or to protect the health of particular individuals or the general public. Statutory requirements are likely to cover some of the disclosures that are needed to protect public safety, but may not cover them all.[4]
- Informing the police that a patient who legitimately possesses a firearm may pose a risk to the public because of an addiction or medical condition.[14]

Summary

- Confidential information may be disclosed, without consent, if doing so is in the public interest.
- Public interest has not been defined by parliament or the courts. Examples of interests that may be sufficient to justify breaching confidentiality include the detection or prevention of crime, the prevention or control of a disease outbreak, and the maintenance of public safety or civil order.

- As each case must be determined on its own merits, the exception is quite uncertain.
- Enacting more mandatory reporting legislation can reduce this uncertainty, but determining what to include in it can be controversial.
- Doctors faced with difficult public interest situations must have access to useful and timely advice.
- Despite its flexibility, the application of the public interest exception is quite restricted, preventing it becoming too broad.

References

1 General Medical Council (2000) *Confidentiality: protecting and providing information*. GMC, London.

2 British Medical Association (1999) *Confidentiality and Disclosure of Health Information*. BMA, London.

3 General Medical Council (2002) *Research: the role and responsibility of doctors*. GMC, London.

4 Department of Health (DoH) (2002) *Confidentiality: a code of practice for NHS staff (draft)*. (www.nhsia.nhs.uk/confidentiality/pages/consultation/docs/code_prac.pdf). (Accessed 24 June 2003.)

5 Cozens C and Milmo D (2002) Campbell privacy case thrown out. *Guardian Unlimited*, 14 October. (http://media.guardian.co.uk/presspublishing/story/0,7495,811789,00.html). (Accessed 3 June 2003.)

6 (2003) In brief – Naomi Campbell case appeal. *Guardian Unlimited*, 28 February. (www.guardian.co.uk/uk_news/story/0,3604,904468,00.html). (Accessed 3 June 2003.)

7 Cambridge Health Informatics Limited (2001) *Gaining Patient Consent to Disclosure*. (www.doh.gov.uk/ipu/confiden/gpcd/exec/gpcdexec.pdf). (Accessed 13 March 2003.)

8 Department of Health (DoH) (2001) *Building the Information Core: protecting and using confidential patient information – a strategy for the NHS*. (www.doh.gov.uk/ipu/confiden/strategyv7.pdf). (Accessed 10 June 2003.)

9 Brown P (2000) Cancer registries fear imminent collapse. *British Medical Journal*. **321**: 854.

10 The Family Violence Prevention Fund (2002) *National Consensus Guidelines on Identifying and Responding to Domestic Violence Victimization in Health Care Settings*. (http://endabuse.org/programs/healthcare/files/Consensus.pdf). (Accessed 3 June 2003.)

11 Cottingham R (2001) Proposals for community violence prevention are naive. *British Medical Journal.* **322**: 677.

12 Department of Health (undated) *Proposal to Revise Regulations made under Section 60 of the Health and Social Care Act 2001.* (www.doh.gov.uk/ipu/act/nhs_databases_consultation_paper.pdf). (Accessed 10 November 2003.)

13 General Medical Council (1997) *Serious Communicable Diseases.* GMC, London.

14 British Medical Association (1996) *Interim Firearms Guidance Note.* BMA, London.

Chapter 9

Legal proceedings – a threat to medical record privacy?

Law enforcement agencies and judicial bodies have various powers to compel the disclosure of medical records for the purpose of criminal investigations and legal proceedings. Although some of these disclosures may benefit patients, and may even be at their request, they often will be strongly resisted. In such situations, a conflict emerges between patients' right to privacy and the need to ensure that justice is not frustrated through lack of relevant information. Where should the line be drawn between access and privacy in legal proceedings?

Using medical records in legal proceedings

The information contained in medical records can be relevant to a wide range of different types of legal disputes. Most commonly, they are used in personal injury claims and negligence actions against doctors and health authorities. In these types of cases, the medical record is often the best documentary evidence of the plaintiff's injuries or the treatment he or she received, and is therefore directly relevant to the issues in dispute. As a result, the use of medical records in cases of this kind tends not to raise any privacy concerns.

Much more contentious is the use of medical records in legal disputes in which a patient's physical or mental health or history has potential relevance to one or more of the matters being considered, but is not a core issue to be determined. In an assault trial, for example, hospital records documenting the complainant's injuries, and anything he or she said about the cause of those injuries at the time of treatment, may be relevant. Although the record does not provide direct evidence that the assault occurred or that it was committed by the accused, it may corroborate (or discredit) the complainant's testimony. Equally, in custody proceedings, past health records documenting substance abuse or mental health problems often are used to cast doubt upon one parent's reliability or capacity to care for the children.

Such tactics are becoming increasingly common, with 36% of family lawyers in Canada reporting that they use health records in half or more of their cases, and a further 41% claiming to use them regularly or occasionally.[1] This is not necessarily a positive or appropriate trend.

A medical record does not automatically constitute good evidence merely because it relates to, or has some bearing on, an incident that is the subject matter of litigation. This is partly because medical records are compiled for health, not legal, purposes.[1] A patient's description of an abusive event in a counselling session, for example, is not provided as evidence of what actually happened, but as part of the process of making sense of his or her feelings, and consequently may not be correct in every factual detail. For example, the tendency for abuse victims to blame themselves could distort the way in which they describe their feelings during counselling. In any event, a counselling record is not a verbatim account of the therapy session but a record of the healthcare provider's interpretation of what was discussed, which includes their biases, clinical observations and speculations.[2] Even in more factual areas, such as the recording of injuries, information documented for a medical purpose can be misleading when used as legal evidence. Injuries relevant to legal proceedings, such as minor scratches and bruises, may have little medical significance and consequently not be noted down.[1]

It is also unclear how much weight should be attributed to the absence of information from a patient's record.* It is tempting, for example, to infer from the fact that no evidence of abuse was recorded that the alleged incident did not take place. This, however, ignores the fact that victims often withhold such information, particularly where domestic violence is involved. This problem may explain why, in the majority of cases involving the abuse of women, the use of medical records tends to be more harmful than helpful to the complainant's case.[1]

Despite these concerns, health records continue to be used routinely in both civil and criminal proceedings (*see* Box 9.1 on p. 126). This can have a significant impact on the confidentiality of medical records and, ultimately, patients' privacy.

---

* For example, in Canada, the fact that a social worker's record did not refer to the alleged sexual assault was held to be consistent with recent fabrication of the event by the complainant (R v Bird (1999) 185 Sask R 102, affirmed (2000) SKCA 72).

Confidentiality and legal proceedings

Discovering the truth requires access to all relevant information. Although patients may sometimes consent to their medical records being used in legal proceedings, they are unlikely to be so agreeable where the record is detrimental to their case, or is required in proceedings to which they are not a party. For this reason, courts (including Coroners' Courts) and some statutory bodies (e.g. the General Medical Council (GMC) and the NHS Complaints Tribunal) have the power to access confidential information, including medical records, despite patients' or healthcare providers' objections, if the information is relevant to a matter before them. Disclosure pursuant to such an order does not breach either the Data Protection Act 1998 or the duty of confidentiality.*

Documents in the control of one of the actual parties involved in a case are obtained through special court processes known as the rules of disclosure.** These rules require each side to disclose to the other all documents upon which they intend to rely, and, upon request, to provide access to documents in their possession. Privileged information, however, need not be disclosed. (*See* definition of 'privileged information' in the 'Glossary of Legal Terms' at the end of this chapter.)

People who are not involved in the proceedings may also be required to produce documents or give oral evidence. If they are not willing to do this voluntarily, the court may, by issuing a witness summons, order them to do so if it is satisfied that the information is relevant and disclosure is appropriate.† Failure to comply with such an order constitutes contempt of court, which is punishable by fine or imprisonment.

This power can be used to compel doctors to produce documents or give evidence in the same way as any other person, even where the information being sought is confidential. The only information protected from disclosure is that which falls within one of the categories of information that have been declared privileged by statute or the common law.[3] Some examples of privileged information include communications between solicitors and their clients, communications between spouses, and confidential government

---

* Data Protection Act 1998, Section 35. *See also* Sections 29 and 31.
** In civil proceedings, this is required by the Civil Procedure Rules, Part 31. In criminal proceedings a roughly similar scheme operates under the Criminal Procedure and Investigations Act 1996, Part 1.
† In civil proceedings, this is done under the Civil Procedure Rules, Part 24. In criminal proceedings, the order is made under the Criminal Procedure (Attendance of Witnesses) Act 1965, Section 2, as amended by the Criminal Procedure and Investigations Act 1996.

documents, the release of which would threaten national security. Medical information, though personal and sensitive, is not privileged.*

This does not mean, however, that patient privacy is ignored, as there are still a number of rules and restrictions that limit the extent to which confidential information can be used in legal proceedings. The first of these comes from the general rule that information will only be received as evidence if it is both relevant and admissible.[4] To be relevant, the information must have a real bearing on the issues to be determined, not just a vague connection to the subject matter of the proceedings. For example, although rape-counselling records contain information relating to the alleged crime, they will not always be relevant to the issues in dispute, as they are only marginally concerned with the detail of what happened, being more focused on patients' feelings.[2] This relevance requirement also means that the court may require disclosure of some parts of a document but not others.[5] This is particularly likely to arise in the case of medical records, as they often contain a wide range of information. Certain information also may be protected from disclosure because it is considered inadmissible, as it breaches one or more of the rules of evidence. Under these rules, for example, documents cannot be accessed if they are intended to be used for the sole purpose of cross-examination, rather than to support the testimony of the requesting party's own witnesses.**

Even where medical information is both relevant and admissible, it may still be possible to resist disclosure on the basis of 'public interest privilege'. This privilege protects against the disclosure of information held by government departments, agencies and statutory bodies where doing so would damage the public interest. For the privilege to apply, the public interest being served by withholding the documents must be so compelling that it outweighs the strong public interest in ensuring that the administration of justice is not frustrated by the absence of relevant information. For example, this privilege was successfully raised by the National Society for the Prevention of Cruelty to Children to avoid naming the informant behind a child abuse allegation.[†] The court was satisfied that there was a strong public interest in ensuring suspicions of child abuse continue to be reported, which would be threatened if anonymity were not assured.

As there is no predetermined limit on the types of situations in which the public interest privilege will be recognised, it could, in theory, be used to

---

* Duchess of Kingston's case (1776) 20 State trials 335; Attorney-General v Mulholland [1963] 2 QB 477; McHale J. Paper on Confidentiality and Mental Health, paper commissioned by the Department of Health for the Mental Health Act Review, 2000. (www.doh.gov.uk/pub/docs/doh/mhapaper.pdf. Accessed 20 May 2003.)
** R v Crown Court at Manchester, ex parte Williams (1985) RTR 49.
† D v National Society for the Prevention of Cruelty to Children (1978) AC 171.

resist the disclosure of medical records held by NHS trusts.* In practice, however, it is likely to be difficult to identify an adequate public interest in this context, as the confidentiality of information is not, by itself, a sufficient consideration. Confidentiality will only support the privilege if maintaining it is the only way to ensure that some other public interest is fulfilled,** which will usually not be the case for medical records. It would be difficult, for example, to prove that using a medical record in one lawsuit would deter other patients from seeking medical care in the future. Medical researchers, on the other hand, may be able to show that disclosing confidential information about a group of research participants would make it difficult for them to secure volunteers in the future, particularly where highly sensitive conditions or genetic factors are being investigated, and the potential subject pool is limited.

Two key considerations when determining whether the public interest in withholding documents should prevail over the need to have all relevant information available are the nature and seriousness of the interests at stake, and the gravity of interference with the patient's privacy.† Disclosure will nearly always be required where the outcome of the proceedings is particularly important, such as a child custody dispute[5] or a criminal trial where the accused's liberty is at stake.‡ In a civil action only involving a claim for damages, however, it may be acceptable to withhold certain documents where their disclosure would interfere with a patient's privacy substantially.§ The court also is more likely to allow confidentiality to prevail if the information is only of minor relevance to the outcome of the trial, only relates to a peripheral issue, or is available from another source.§

Where confidential information does need to be disclosed under a legal order, healthcare providers should, of course, continue to be mindful of their confidentiality obligations, and only disclose the information strictly in accordance with its terms.[6] As the order provides the legal justification for breaching confidentiality, any disclosure above and beyond its terms is both a breach of the Data Protection Act 1998 and of doctors' ethical obligations. The importance of adhering to the terms of the order is well illustrated by the case of a Canadian physician who was held to have breached confidentiality

---

*D v National Society for the Prevention of Cruelty to Children (1978) AC 171, per Lord Hailsham of St Marylebone at 605.
** D v National Society for the Prevention of Cruelty to Children (1978) AC 171, per Lord Simon of Glaisdale at 612. In the NSPCC case, the public interest served by maintaining confidentiality was the need to encourage child abuse reporting.
† Z v Finland (1998) 25 EHRR 371.
‡ Re M (A Minor) (Disclosure of Material) (1990) 2 FLR 36 (discussed in the context of social worker logs); Conway v Rimmer (1968) AC 910.
§ A (M) v Ryan (1997) 1 SCR 157 (Supreme Court of Canada).

by releasing parts of a patient's medical record that related to a time period outside that specified in the relevant court order.* Where appropriate, it is also good practice to inform patients of the requested disclosure before it is made or as soon as possible thereafter.[6]

Should there be a medical professional privilege?

The growing interest in protecting medical privacy has led to renewed calls for the UK to recognise an official 'medical privilege', exempting medical records and other patient information from disclosure in legal proceedings. Support for this idea comes from the fact that 'privilege' is extended to other types of information, much of which is less confidential and sensitive than that contained in medical records,** without any apparent damage to the delivery of justice. For example, privilege attaches to discussions between lawyers and their clients, even though legal information is usually less private and intimate than medical information and its disclosure less embarrassing. This argument, however, is based on a misconception as to the rationale for recognising privilege.

The absence or existence of a professional privilege is not recognition of the importance of the profession, the value of the information discussed within the professional relationship, or even the personal and sensitive nature of the information in question. In determining whether to recognise a particular class of privilege, the primary consideration is the purpose it will serve.[7] Legal professional privilege, for example, which applies to documents prepared for legal proceedings, is considered necessary for the effective operation of the legal system, as it ensures clients can receive advice without jeopardising their legal position or threatening their right to a fair trial.[†] The disclosure of medical information, on the other hand, is unlikely to jeopardise the patient's, or anyone else's, legal position. The existence of legal professional privilege, therefore, does not support the case for recognising a medical privilege.

The real issue to consider is whether the value of recognising medical privilege outweighs the harm that the deprivation of medical information

---

* Mammone v Bakan (1989) BCT No. 2438.
** For example, 'without prejudice' communications (Rabin v Mendoza & Co (1954) 1 All ER 247); discussions between a lawyer and his or her client in anticipation of legal proceedings (Balabel v Air India (1988) 2 All ER 246); the identity of an informant to the Gaming Board for Great Britain (Rogers v Secretary of State for the Home Department (1972) 2 All ER 1057).
† D v National Society for the Prevention of Cruelty to Children (1978) AC 171, per Lord Simon of Glaisdale at 606.

will cause to the search for the truth. The answer is likely to be no. The embarrassment and emotional and financial harm that can result from using medical records in legal proceedings are not sufficient reasons for withholding important evidence, particularly as the magnitude of harm can be minimised by limiting the extent to which the evidence is made available to the public (*see* 'Safeguards' p. 123). There is also no conclusive evidence that the absence of a medical privilege deters people from seeking medical treatment or being candid with their doctor.* Studies investigating this possibility in the context of mental health and counselling services have found that people are generally unaware of the legal rules relating to privilege, and their behaviour is therefore little affected by them.[9]** It is unclear, however, whether behavioural changes would be seen if they were informed of the rules.

Even in some of the jurisdictions that do recognise medical privilege, its value has been questioned. The task force reviewing the rules of evidence in Victoria, Australia, for example, was unable to find a convincing rationale for the existence of the medical privilege that exists in that state and recommended it be abolished.[8] Although the task force recognised that the confidentiality of doctor–patient communications should sometimes be respected, a blanket privilege was not considered the best way of achieving this. This view is supported by the leading Australian text on the law of privilege, which found that the Victorian legislation has given rise to many uncertainties:

> *The privilege has rarely operated effectively in protecting a patient's interest in making full and frank disclosure to his or her doctor. In fact, the few cases where the privilege has been claimed have given rise to conflicts in interpretation and doubts as to ... [its] scope.*[11]

This view is supported by numerous examples of the privilege having excluded evidence of great importance, increasing the potential for incorrect decisions.† Even the Victorian judiciary has criticised the privilege,

---

* According to the Commonwealth Attorney-General's Department in Australia, there is 'no reason to believe that the absence of a privilege has any adverse effect on the nature, extent or quality of medical services' (Appendix A – Letter from the Commonwealth Attorney-General's Department, dated 7 February 1996).[8]

** This finding is consistent with studies showing that the Tarasoff decision in the USA (which held that therapists have a duty to warn individuals who are at risk from a patient under their care) had little impact on patient behaviour.[10]

† For example, medical records, which would show whether a deceased patient had suffered from a disease he allegedly had concealed to obtain a life insurance policy, were excluded in an action under the policy (Warnecke v Equitable Life Assurance Society of the United States (1906) VLR 482); a doctor's evidence of bodily characteristics observed during consultation was excluded in an action to annul a marriage on the ground of impotence, despite the fact that it would corroborate the petitioner's case (F (otherwise M) v F (1950) VLR 352).

describing the exclusion of all information a medical advisor acquires as placing 'an obstruction in the way of the investigation of truth, which has no – or, at any rate, an utterly inadequate – compensatory advantage'.*

Given these problems, it is not surprising that most jurisdictions that recognise medical privilege have limited its operation. In Victoria, the privilege only exists in civil, not criminal, proceedings.** In most states in the USA it only applies to psychotherapists, not the general medical profession, and is subject to a number of exceptions.[2]

In the light of these experiences, it is unlikely to be beneficial for the UK to establish an official medical privilege. This does not mean, however, that the current way of using medical records in legal proceedings does not need careful scrutiny. Although there are many examples of courts recognising, and giving weight to, the importance of privacy, medical records also have been accessed for questionable purposes (*see* pp 124–5). It is vital that the judiciary be aware of the consequences of disclosing medical records in legal proceedings and vigilant to misuses of the discovery process. Patient privacy should be given considerable weight when determining both the extent and manner in which medical information is used.

Patients' privacy also can be protected by ensuring that anyone affected by an order to disclose medical records for legal proceedings receives notice of that order, thus enabling them to voice their concerns. In the UK, a copy of the order need only be provided to the person in control of the requested documents, who then has seven days in which to lodge objections.[†] Frequently, healthcare providers fail to take advantage of this right to object, either because of time pressures or a reluctance to become involved in legal processes.[‡] Although affected patients are entitled to raise objections themselves, they often are deprived the opportunity to do so, not having been informed of the order's existence. By contrast, in sexual offence cases in Canada, applications for the disclosure of records must not only be given to the judge, but also to the prosecution, to the third party in possession of the record, to the complainant or witness, and to any other party to whom, to the knowledge of the accused, the record relates.[§] This ensures that all interested

---

*Warnecke v Equitable Life Assurance Society of the United States (1906) VLR 482, per Hodges J at 488. This criticism has been endorsed in subsequent decisions, such as Andasteel Constructions Pty Ltd v Taylor (1964) VR 112.
**Evidence Act 1958 (Vic), Section 28.
[†] Crown Court Rules 1982, Rule 23.
[‡] In a review of Canadian assault cases by the Woman Abuse Response Program, very few of the health authorities were found to have objected to disclosure orders, with those that did rarely having legal representation. Interestingly, in R v Baker (1995) NJ No. 318 (Prov. Ct.), one of the few cases where a health authority did obtain legal representation formally to oppose the disclosure, the authority's objection was successful.[1]
[§] Canadian Criminal Code, Section 278.3(5). A similar notice requirement for sexual assault cases exists in New South Wales, Australia (Evidence Act 1995 (NSW), Section 126 (as

parties have an opportunity to make their objections known. Arguably, the UK would benefit more from changes of this kind than from adopting a formal medical privilege.

Safeguards

Using a medical record in legal proceedings will always interfere with patients' privacy to some degree. However, it need not result in the information becoming public knowledge.[8] Unless there is a pressing reason not to, 'the manner, mode and extent of disclosure should be such as to impair the right to privacy as little as possible'.[2] There are a number of methods by which this can be done.

First, before making confidential documents available to the parties, the judge can conduct a closed inspection of the documents to remove any unimportant or irrelevant communications.[5] This reduces the amount of confidential information that will be disclosed at the trial. The court then can enter an order in respect of any information that is made available, preventing its disclosure to anyone other than the parties, their counsels, relevant expert witnesses and the court.* The parties usually have to destroy or return all copies of the information once it is no longer required for the purpose of the trial. It is also possible to close the court to the public and media, either for the entire trial or, more commonly, during the periods in which confidential information is to be discussed.**

The benefit of these types of safeguards is well illustrated by Z v Finland,[†] which involved a complaint by an HIV-positive woman against her medical records being used, without her permission, in legal proceedings against her husband. The wife's medical records were considered relevant to determining when her husband, who was accused of intentionally infecting others with HIV, first became aware of his condition. The European Court of Human Rights accepted that the seriousness of the issues at stake meant that some interference with the wife's privacy was necessary and that, for the most part, the extent of the interference was appropriately limited by the use of safeguards. It was acceptable to have seized her medical records, used

amended) and Criminal Procedure Amendment (Sexual Assault Communications Privilege) Act 1999, Schedule 1).
* For example, Z v Finland (1998) 25 EHRR 371; Farnsworth v Proctor & Gamble Company 758 F2d 1545 (11th circuit, 1985).
** Scott v Scott (1913) AC 417.
[†] Z v Finland (1988) 25 EHRR 371.

them at trial, and compelled her doctors to give evidence about her, as the evidence was given in non-public court sessions and appropriate confidentiality orders were made. Her privacy was breached, however, when her name and HIV status were included in the court's judgement. The interests of justice could have been served without interfering with her privacy, by the court exercising its discretion to omit names from the judgement or by publishing an abridged version of its reasoning.

Misuse of legal processes

Although medical records often contain valuable evidence, and usually are used for valid purposes, the ability to access this type of information can be misused. A common example of this is the submission of speculative disclosure applications.[2] In what are known as 'fishing expeditions', lawyers demand access to private documents, with little knowledge of their potential relevance, in the hope that they will chance upon useful evidence. Courts do not look favourably upon such tactics, and are likely to reject applications that are not sufficiently specific or fail to demonstrate the potential relevance of the requested documents, particularly where confidential information is involved. The risk remains, however, that some questionable applications will slip through, particularly if healthcare providers do not object to the request. It is difficult to assess the extent to which this occurs, or the prevalence of other inappropriate disclosure orders, but some concerning isolated examples have been reported.*

For this reason, some jurisdictions have created special statutory safeguards to restrict the discovery process in relation to particularly sensitive types of information. Legislation regulating sexual assault cases in Canada, for example, reinforces the usual requirement that applicants demonstrate the relevance of documents they request, by listing a number of assertions which, on their own, will not be considered sufficient evidence of relevance.** These include the fact that a record relates to an incident that is the subject matter of the proceedings or that relates to the complainant's sexual reputation. Whilst common law procedures and principles can be just as effective at excluding this type of evidence, formal legislation may help discourage the submission of inappropriate applications, and reinforce the

---

* For example, a UK court ordered an NHS trust to disclose the address of a woman to enable divorce papers to be served on her. (Reported by Marlene Winfield, Head of Patient and Citizen Relations, NHS Information Authority, during discussions with Heidi Tranberg in London on 31 March 2003.)
** Canadian Criminal Code, Section 278.3(4).

sensitivity of certain types of records and the need for a compelling reason to exist before it is appropriate to compromise patients' privacy. Even if legislation of this type is not required, it would be useful to have clearer guidelines about the disclosures that courts should and should not order to ensure its processes are not abused to the detriment of individual privacy.

Of even more concern, and much more difficult to control, is the potential for litigants to use confidential medical information accessed through the court processes as a means of harassment, or to use the threat of further disclosure to force a settlement.[7] This is particularly likely to occur where the parties know each other, and therefore each other's medical histories, very well.[1] A party also could use their knowledge of the existence of certain records acquired in one set of proceedings to obtain access to additional records in separate legal action.* As reports of such practices tend to be anecdotal only, it is difficult to assess the prevalence of this problem.

Conclusion

The use of medical records in legal proceedings can be distressing and embarrassing for patients, but often it is necessary to ensure justice is served. For this reason, recognising a formal medical privilege is unlikely to be the best way of regulating the use of medical records in litigation. Instead, the courts must be vigilant about what disclosures they order, with both healthcare providers and patients being given sufficient notice of relevant applications to enable them to make their objections known. Where it is necessary to access patient information, the manner and extent of disclosure should be designed to minimise the degree of interference with the patient's privacy.

---

*For example, the accused in a criminal trial seeking access to the complainant's records in a later civil trial (R v ER (2000) OJ No. 5083 (Court of Justice); R v White (1998) 132 CCC (3d) 373 (Ontario Court of Appeal)).

Box 9.1

Examples of requests for, and uses of, medical documents in legal proceedings

- In a public liability action against a tampon manufacturer, the plaintiffs, who claimed to have been injured by toxic shock syndrome, submitted, as part of their evidence, independent research findings regarding the syndrome. The manufacturer sought access to the names and addresses of the research participants in order to discover biases in the methodology. The court allowed the disclosure subject to a number of protective measures, such as restricting access to the parties' legal teams, requiring confidentiality undertakings from the recipients, and ordering the return of the data at the end of the proceedings.*
- In a criminal assault trial, the court interpreted the absence of any reference to the alleged incident in a social worker's record as being consistent with the complainant having fabricated the allegations.**
- A subpoena was issued to a number of fertility clinics in Iowa, requiring the disclosure of the names and addresses of all women who had received a positive pregnancy test during a specified period, to assist the police in identifying who had abandoned a dead foetus. One clinic opposed the subpoena on the basis that it would distress those who had lost a foetus or newborn, and damage trust in the doctor–patient relationship. The relevance of the information also was queried, as there was no evidence that the mother actually lived in the area. The matter was resolved when the original order for the release of the information, made by the District Court of Iowa, was withdrawn, following the commencement of an appeal to the Iowa Supreme Court.[12]
- In a sexual assault case, the complainant's psychiatric records were discussed in open court without her knowledge. As a result, and to her distress, private information became known to those members of her family who were seated in the public gallery.
- Fears have been expressed about the possibility of defendants in future personal injury claims being given access to the plaintiff's genetic data. Genetic evidence that the plaintiff's life expectancy is shorter than that of the average person could be used to reduce the award of future damages that he or she would otherwise receive.[13] To date, there are no reports of this having occurred.

---

* Farnsworth v Procter & Gamble Company 758 F2d 1545 (11th circuit, 1985).
** R v Bird (1999) 185 Sask R 102, affirmed (2000) SKCA 72.

Glossary of legal terms

- *Admissible*. Evidence is admissible if the trial judge decides that it:
  - will help the jury (or, in cases that do not involve a jury, the judge) determine the facts
  - is not irrelevant or immaterial
  - does not breach any of the rules of evidence.
- *Contempt of court*. A judge can declare a person to be in contempt of court if they wilfully fail to obey an order of the court, or are rude or disruptive in the court room (usually after having been warned not to act in that way). The normal punishment for contempt of court is a fine, but it also can result in short periods of imprisonment.
- *Party*. A person, corporation or other legal entity that files a lawsuit (e.g. plaintiff or petitioner) or defends against one (e.g. defendant or respondent).
- *Privileged information*. Information that belongs to one of a number of special classes of information that is exempt from disclosure in legal proceedings. For example, a document prepared by a lawyer for the purpose of legal proceedings, information that is subject to a statutory provision imposing secrecy, such as certain records relating to adopted children, and a document that the parties previously agreed would be exempt from disclosure.
- *Public interest*. The well-being of the general public. In a legal context, this term is often contrasted with the needs or interests of a specific person or group of people.
- *Relevant*. Evidence is relevant if it has some tendency to prove a matter of fact significant to the case.
- *Rules of evidence*. A body of rules that govern whether information can be received into evidence during legal proceedings. For example, the rules of evidence prevent the use of information that was obtained illegally, even though it may be relevant. Graphic photos of a victim's injuries also may be excluded, despite having a clear connection to the case, on the basis that the jury's shock at the gory details will outweigh the photos' evidentiary value.
- *Statutory body*. An organisation, committee or other body of persons established by or under any law, such as NHS trusts, special health authorities, the General Medical Council and the Medical Research Council.
- *Witness summons*. An order of the court for a person to produce specified documents, or appear at a particular time and place to give oral evidence.

Summary:

- Medical records are used regularly in both civil and criminal trials. In some cases they are used inappropriately.
- The court can order healthcare providers to disclose medical records for legal proceedings, despite the fact that they are confidential.
- There is no general medical privilege in the UK, but in exceptional cases it may be possible to withhold medical records on the basis of public interest privilege.
- Introducing medical privilege is not likely to be beneficial. Instead, greater guidance is required as to what disclosures courts should and should not order. When an order is made, notice should be given to all people affected by it, enabling them to raise their objections.
- The impact of the use of medical records in legal proceedings on individual privacy can be minimised in a number of ways.
- The ability to access medical records for legal proceedings is sometimes misused.

References

1 Woman Abuse Response Program (2003) *Reasonable Doubt: the use of health records in legal cases of violence against women in relationships*. British Columbia's Women's Hospital and Health Centre. (www.bcifv.org/resources/reasonabledoubt.html). (Accessed 19 May 2003.)

2 Temkin J (2001) *Comments in Response to the Criminal Courts Review by the Right Honourable Lord Justice Auld*. The Lord Chancellor's Department. (www.lcd.gov.uk/criminal/auldcom/ar/ar5.htm). (Accessed 20 May 2003.)

3 Halsbury's Laws of England *Medicine, Pharmacy, Drugs and Medicinal Products*, paragraph 18.

4 Halsbury's Laws of England *Evidence*, paragraph 409.

5 National Legal Research Group (1995) *Discovery of a Party's Mental Health Records in Child Custody Matters*. Divorce Research Centre. (www.divorcesource.com/research/dl/childcustody/95oct219.shtml). (Accessed 20 May 2003.)

6 British Medical Association (1999) *Confidentiality and Disclosure of Health Information*. BMA, London.

7 Winick B (1996) The psychotherapist–patient privilege: a therapeutic jurisprudence view. *U Miami L Rev*. **50**: 249.

8 Scrutiny of Acts and Regulations Committee (1996) *Review of the Evidence Act 1958 (Vic) and Review of the Role and Appointment of Public Notaries.* Parliament of Victoria. (www.parliament.vic.gov.au/sarc/Evidence%20Report/rea96.html). (Accessed 20 May 2003.)

9 Shuman D and Weiner M (1984) Privilege – a comparative study. *Journal of Psychiatry and Law.* **12**: 373.

10 Beck J (1982) When the patient threatens violence – an empirical study of the clinical practice after Tarasoff. *Bull Am Acad Psychiatry & Law.* **10**: 189.

11 McNicol S (1992) *Law of Privilege.* Law Book Company, Sydney: 395.

12 Planned Parenthood of Greater Iowa (2002) *Planned Parenthood's Medical Privacy Case Dismissed.* (www.ppgi.org/includes/media/proct3102.htm). (Accessed 20 October 2003.)

13 Rothstein M (1997) *Preventing the Discovery of Plaintiff Genetic Profiles by Defendants Seeking to Limit Damages in Personal Injury Litigation.* Indiana University. (http://law.indiana.edu/ilj/v71/no4/rothstei.html). (Accessed 19 May 2003.)

Chapter 10

Anonymous information

Using and disclosing patients' medical information only threatens their privacy if they can be identified from it. Although identifiable information usually is required for the provision of actual care and treatment, this is not always the case for other types of activities. Many of the secondary purposes for which medical records are used, such as research, disease surveillance and planning, require access to individual patient data, but do not require that patients are actually identified. These purposes often can be achieved, therefore, by use of anonymous data. Doing this will not only protect patients' privacy, but also may benefit healthcare providers and data users, as there are less legal restrictions controlling the way this type of data can be used.

Anonymous and pseudonymous data

Patient information usually is recorded in an identifiable form, with most medical records and similar documents containing a huge number and variety of personal identifiers.[1] These identifiers include patients' names or derivatives of it, their personal characteristics (such as date of birth, gender and occupation), contextual information (such as their address and health-related dates) and any number of coded identifiers assigned to them, such as their NHS Number or local patient code.* Even clinical data itself can be quite particular to individuals.[2]

Given the personal nature of this information, making it anonymous can be quite a complex task, involving considerable effort and expertise. Depending upon the purpose for which data are required, the de-identification either can be done completely, creating *anonymous data*, or by replacing patients' identities with a code or pseudonym, creating *pseudonymous data*.

---

*The Caldicott Committee concluded that 'all items of information which related to an attribute of an individual should be treated as potentially capable of identifying patients, to a greater or lesser extent' (paragraph 4.1).[1]

Anonymous data

Information is considered anonymous if there is no reasonable possibility that it can be linked, in the future, with the patient to whom it related.[3] To achieve this standard, all identifiers with potential to reveal patients' identities must be removed or masked.

Carrying out this procedure can be difficult, as the discriminatory power of individual data items cannot be assessed in isolation.[3] Data items that cannot, when considered on their own, identify a patient may well be able to do so when combined with other identifiers in the data, the data user's prior knowledge of the patient, or additional information to which he or she may have access (*see* Chapter 7, p. 93). This can be seen with the identifiers listed above. Although many identifiers are unable to identify a patient on their own, they could enable a patient's identity to be deduced when considered in combination. The potential for this to occur obviously increases as more data items are added to the data set, although with today's powerful search engines and large, interlinked databases, even a small number of identifiers may be sufficient.[2] The increasing amount of publicly available data, much of which is freely and easily accessible on the internet, has also made it easier to identify individuals from seemingly anonymous information.[4]

Pseudonymous data

In pseudonymous data, a patient's true identity is encoded or encrypted to form a pseudonym, which is an arbitrary but consistent code that identifies the patient in the system, but from which their identity cannot readily be recognised in the real world. Thus, whilst only de-identified information appears in the database, the ability to 'unlock' or decode the pseudonym means that the connection between patients and their data is not lost completely.

Maintaining this link between patients and their information can be very useful. It enables data users to combine separate items of data from different sources (such as from medical records and death certificates) and to trace patients' health status over time. The use of pseudonymous data also can help to improve the quality of data sets, as users can check that there are no duplicate entries in the system, and follow up any omissions or apparent inaccuracies with the relevant data provider. It also makes it possible to contact individual patients to obtain further information or pass on important findings.

Pseudonymous data can be designed to be reversible, so that it is possible to re-establish a patient's identity at a later stage, or non-reversible. Both types can be used to link data, provided the process of assigning the pseudonyms is carried out consistently, both across different organisations and over time. For some types of analyses, however, the ability to reverse the pseudonyms will be vital. For example, reversible pseudonyms are usually used in longitudinal and cohort research studies and disease-monitoring activities. Although this can raise additional privacy concerns, both types of pseudonymous data can protect patient privacy adequately, provided two requirements are met.

First, the pseudonym assigned to patients must not itself contain information that could identify them.* It should not, for example, be a simple derivative of a patient's name. Although this may seem obvious, a common way of 'anonymously' presenting real patient cases at clinical meetings has been to replace the patient's name with their initials, a technique unlikely to prevent identification in many instances.

Second, the decoding key must be carefully protected.[3] In some cases, such as NHS numbers, this key will be a simple reference list detailing each patient and their corresponding pseudonym. Alternatively, if patients are assigned pseudonyms via an explicit set of rules, such as an encryption algorithm,** the rules themselves will be the decoding key. In either case, this information must be stored securely, and separately from the identifying data, ideally in a way that prevents those with access to the main data also having access to the key. In the case of reversible pseudonyms, reversals should be allowed only in specific, predetermined circumstances.

If these requirements are met, pseudonymous data provide a reliable basis upon which data items can be linked without revealing patients' identities, although there is still some risk that errors could be made.[3] The system may fail to match pairs of records relating to one individual, or erroneously link records relating to two separate individuals. Whilst this risk exists with all record linkage, whether matches are based on pseudonyms or combinations of personal identifiers, the use of pseudonyms can cause particular problems unless the pseudonymisation process is handled carefully.

A crucial component of this is ensuring that the original, identifiable information to which the pseudonyms are assigned is of a high quality, in that it is complete, accurate and recorded in a consistent manner. In the UK, the potential for errors can be reduced substantially by including the NHS Number on all patient documents, as this is a particularly reliable and unique identifier upon which to base record matches. Having complete and accurate records also minimises the need to reverse pseudonyms (to clarify

---

* Privacy Rule, 45 CFR Section 164.514 (2002).
** An encryption algorithm is a mathematical process that can be used to convert data into a form that cannot be easily understood without access to the algorithm. The algorithm will produce the same pseudonym for a given value of personal identifier.

apparent inconsistencies or obtain additional information), a process that can itself threaten privacy.

As discussed earlier, it is also essential that the pseudonyms be applied consistently. Again the NHS Number, being a uniform identifier already used within the NHS, may be the best way of ensuring this is done. Provided NHS numbers are included on all records and other patient materials, this option also can reduce the cost and effort of assigning pseudonyms.[3]

If these requirements are met, pseudonymous data can be used for many purposes that cannot be achieved using data that is fully anonymous. For this reason, the Department of Health,[5] the Information Commissioner[6] and the General Medical Council[7] all support increasing the extent to which such data are used within the NHS. The best way of creating pseudonymous data, according to the Department of Health, is through the encryption of NHS numbers, a proposal considered in further detail in Box 10.1.

Box 10.1

The NHS Number

The NHS Number is a randomly generated 10-character number (consisting of nine identifiers and one check digit used to confirm the validity of the number) assigned to every individual registered with the NHS in England and Wales. It is used to provide an unambiguous reference point to link patient information across departments and organisations. As NHS numbers are never reused, even after the number holder has died, it is a unique identifier, enabling those dealing with patient information to be confident that they are dealing with the correct patient file.

The NHS Number also provides a level of protection for patient privacy and confidentiality, as it is less likely to reveal patients' identities than more public identifiers, such as names and addresses. The use of NHS numbers, however, does not make data anonymous, as anyone with knowledge of, or access to, a patient's number will be able to establish his or her identity.[8,9] This could include a substantial number of people, as authorised staff within all NHS organisations can access the database of numbers contained in the NHS Central Register. It also is possible for non-NHS organisations to become aware of a specific patient's NHS Number if, for example, it is included on correspondence about the patient that they receive. Identifying patient data through the patient's NHS Number, therefore, is not an adequate method of pseudonymisation.

A much more effective way of protecting patients' privacy, according to the Department of Health, is by using an encrypted version of the NHS Number.[10] To identify a patient from this encrypted code, data users not only need access to the patient's NHS Number, but also the algorithm used to perform the encryption. Provided the algorithm is not made public, the patient's identity is concealed effectively.

The main problem with the use of NHS numbers as the basis for pseudonymising data is the fact that they are yet to be universally used on all patient records and correspondence. Despite the recommendation of the Caldicott Committee in 1997 that the use of NHS numbers be increased,[1] this information is still absent from many medical records. The number of records containing NHS numbers actually declined from 2000 to 2001.[11] It also can be difficult to trace the numbers belonging to some groups of people, such as the homeless, whereas other users of the NHS, such as foreign visitors, may not have been assigned one.[11]

Acceptable levels of anonymity

Making data anonymous and pseudonymous may seem straightforward, but achieving an acceptable level of anonymity, sufficient to ensure that patients cannot be identified from the data, can actually be quite difficult. Data can fall along a spectrum of identifiability, as outlined in Box 10.2 on p. 144. Obviously, the most effective way of protecting patients' privacy is to remove each and every personal identifier contained in the information. Depending upon the purpose for which the information is required, however, it may not be possible to do this completely. Dates of birth and places of residence, for example, which are both capable of revealing patients' identities when combined with other information, are key variables analysed in many research and disease-monitoring projects. The same is true for hospital admission and discharge dates, which are often relevant in administrative and service planning activities.

In cases like these, where one or more identifiers need to be retained, it is often possible to reduce the particular variable's power of identification by truncation or rounding.[3] Dates of birth can usually be reformatted to a 'mm/yyyy' form, for example, without adversely affecting the analyses being conducted. Equally, where geographical factors are relevant, it may be possible to use standard zones, such as electoral wards, or postcodes that have been abbreviated to sector level, rather than full, individual postcodes.

Even with these techniques, there will always be some data sets that cannot be made anonymous to an acceptable level. Despite the information having been de-identified as far as possible, there may still be a reasonable risk that a patient's identity could be deduced. In some cases this is because the activity being conducted requires access to fairly specific information. Alternatively, the information simply may be so unusual that removing the types of identifiers that normally would make a data set anonymous will not be sufficient to protect a patient's identity completely.[12] For example, whilst it usually would be difficult to identify a patient knowing only their medical condition and city of residence, this could be possible if their condition was particularly uncommon for that area, or was already in the public domain, as for example an accident involving a known personality. This problem is made all the more difficult by the existence of numerous, unresolved issues concerning the legal status of anonymous data.

Legal status

The Data Protection Act 1998 and the duty of confidentiality are only concerned with information that is capable of identifying the individual to whom it relates.* Information that has been made anonymous, therefore, can be used and disclosed without reference to these restrictions. This has been affirmed by the Court of Appeal in a recent decision concerning the purchase of anonymous pharmacy prescription information by Source Informatics, a company that supplies information about doctors' prescribing habits to drug manufacturers.** According to the Court, the principal concern of the law in this context is the protection of personal privacy. Provided the patient's identity is concealed, therefore, disclosing this information is not considered a breach of confidentiality. The Court's opinion was not altered by the fact that, in the Source Informatics situation, the information originally was provided for the sole purpose of enabling the pharmacist to dispense drugs.

Strictly speaking, the Court of Appeal's decision only relates to the impact of anonymity on the duty of confidentiality, as the decision pre-dated the commencement of the Data Protection Act 1998. Comments made by the Court, however, suggest that the same result would be reached under the

---

* The Data Protection Act only applies to 'personal data', which is defined as 'data which relate to a living individual who can be identified from those data or from those data and other information which is in the possession of, or likely to come into the possession of, the data controller'. (Data Protection Act 1998, Section 1(1).)

** R v Department of Health, ex parte Source Informatics Ltd (2000) 1 All ER 786.

Act.* Notwithstanding this, the decision still leaves unresolved a number of issues regarding the legal status of de-identified data.

The Court's findings were based on the assumption that there was no risk that patients could be identified from the information, a standard that will not be met in the vast majority of cases. As discussed above, de-identification usually only reduces the risk that an individual can be identified, often to an extremely low level, not eliminates it entirely. Before healthcare providers and data users can rely with confidence on the anonymity of patient data to avoid the obligations of the Data Protection Act 1998, therefore, they need to determine whether a sufficient level of anonymity has been achieved.[2] That is, they need to assess whether the data has been 'acceptably anonymised'.[13] There is currently little legal guidance to help them make this judgement.[13]

In the Source Informatics case, patients' names and addresses were removed from the prescription data before being disclosed, leaving only the name of the prescribing doctor, the product and quantity prescribed, and the dates on which the prescription was made and the product dispensed. Although the judge in the original trial expressed some concern over the risk that, despite this process, patients could still be identified from the information, he accepted that on the facts before him there was no evidence 'which sets out any rational basis for such concerns'.** Ultimately, both at trial and on appeal, the case was decided on the assumption that anonymity would be guaranteed. As a consequence, the Court did not provide any guidance as to the types of identifiers that need to be removed for information to be classed as sufficiently anonymous, nor what will be considered an acceptable risk of identification. The Source Informatics case also left open the issue of whether pseudonymous data has the same legal status as that which is fully anonymous. Although it seems reasonable to view it this way, provided re-identification is strictly controlled, this argument is yet to be subject to a test of legality.

In the absence of clear legal rules as to what constitutes 'acceptably anonymised' data, healthcare professionals using or disclosing apparently anonymous patient information risk the possibility of a legal challenge.[14] To overcome this problem, NHS Scotland recommends that the concept of 'acceptably anonymised' be defined by legislation.[13] The definition could either set out a specific standard of anonymity with which the information must conform, or establish a clearance process, such as an ethics committee examination and approval, through which the data must pass.

---

*R v Department of Health, ex parte Source Informatics Ltd (2000) 1 All ER 786, per Simon Brown LJ at 797–8.
** R v Department of Health, ex parte Source Informatics Ltd (1999) 4 All ER 185, per Latham J at 196.

Legislation of this kind already exists in the USA. Under its Federal Privacy Rule, data are considered sufficiently de-identified if either a qualified statistician makes a formal determination to this effect, or all the identifiers listed in the legislation are removed. Included in this list of identifiers are a patient's (or a relative's, employer's or household member's) name, telephone or fax numbers, email address, social security or medical record number, and 'any other unique identifying number, characteristic or code'.* Geographical locations must not be described any more specifically than state level or through the first three digits of a zip code,** and dates and ages must be expressed as whole years.† The controller of the data also must not have actual knowledge that would allow the remaining information, alone or in combination with other information, to identify an individual.‡

The legislation also clarifies that pseudonymous data are considered anonymous provided the pseudonyms are not derived from identifiable information and the decoding key is not available to data users.§ As 'unique identifying numbers' are classified as potential identifiers, pseudonyms could not be based on US social security numbers (or NHS numbers in the UK), although it should be acceptable to use an encrypted form of these numbers.

Although there are currently no plans to enact similar legislation in the UK, the Department of Health is investigating the potential to make greater use of anonymous and pseudonymous data. As part of this investigation it has developed a draft 'pseudonymisation toolkit', which is designed to assist healthcare providers and data users to manage the process by helping them identify the highest level of anonymity or pseudonymity that will meet the data requirements of individual studies and projects.[3,15] The toolkit classifies information as anonymous if the probability of an individual being identified from it is minimal, the example being one in a million.¶ Pseudonymous

---

*It is acceptable to include pseudonyms in a data set, provided they comply with the requirements set out in the Rule (Privacy Rule, 45 CFR Section 164.514(b) (2002)).
**Provided the area covered by the first three digits of the zip code includes more than 20 000 people (Privacy Rule, 45 CFR Section 164.514(b) (2002)).
† All ages over 89 must be removed or aggregated into a single '90 years or over' category (Privacy Rule, 45 CFR Section 164.514(b) (2002)).
‡ Privacy Rule, 45 CFR Section 164.514(b) (2002).
§ Privacy Rule, 45 CFR Section 164.514(c) (2002). The data can only be disclosed under an agreement in which the recipient, among other things, specifies their intended uses and disclosures, names who will be using the data, commits to certain safeguards, and agrees not to attempt to identify or contact the patients.
¶ Similar standards have been expressed in ethical guidelines. For example, though the British Medical Association acknowledges that aggregating data may be the only way of making it truly anonymous, it does not consider such a high standard of anonymity to be necessary from an ethical perspective.[16]

data can fall within this definition provided safeguards are in place to protect the decoding key.

Who should make data anonymous?

The process of making identifiable data anonymous or pseudonymous can be extremely time-consuming. Considerable work is required to detect and extract potentially identifying information from each data set and, if necessary, assign pseudonyms. The amount and type of information that needs to be removed or truncated for each project will differ depending upon the nature of the information involved and the purpose for which it is to be used. Consequently, even where electronic records allow some of this process to be automated, a degree of manual work and personal judgement still may be required. For long-term projects, the costs not only involve the initial expense of preparing the original data and assigning pseudonyms, but also the continuing cost of inputting new information and dealing with requests for reversals. A major aspect of deciding to use anonymous information, therefore, is determining who should perform and pay for the anonymisation work. The Department of Health has examined a number of alternatives.[3]

The first option is for healthcare providers to make data anonymous or pseudonymous themselves, before releasing it to data users. This avoids the need for any additional disclosures of identifiable data, increasing the protection of patients' privacy. By having a direct relationship between data providers and data users, without the addition of any intermediary organisation, this approach also has the potential to be quite efficient. To work successfully, however, the relevant healthcare providers must have the resources, skills and experience needed to undertake the work. Often, this will not be the case, particularly where small general practice surgeries are involved or the work includes large volumes of data or complex pseudonymisation. In any event, having to carry out this task will increase the workload of an already overworked group. This could deter some healthcare providers from agreeing to supply information to third parties, which could have a significant impact on the quantity and quality of data that is available for secondary purposes. This approach, therefore, is unlikely to be appropriate for most large-scale projects.

For work that is sizeable, complex or involves the pooling of information from a number of different sources, it may be more appropriate for the process of making data anonymous to be managed by some type of specialised intermediary service. The intermediary service would be responsible for making anonymous (or pseudonymous) identifiable information received from healthcare providers before passing it on to data users. The intermediary also would deal with any queries or requests from data users, including contacting the original healthcare provider, where necessary. As a specialist service, the intermediary should have the skills and resources needed to perform this work to a high standard, ensuring that the process is effective and consistent. As this approach involves the disclosure of identifiable information to an additional organisation, however, it raises a number of privacy issues.* By adding an extra 'player' to the anonymity process, it also increases the number and complexity of information exchanges, which may introduce time delays (particularly in responding to requests for the reversal of pseudonyms)** and increase the risk that data will be lost. There also may be considerable costs involved in setting up and running this type of service.

Given these potential problems, many of those involved in the health industry are sceptical about the benefits of creating an 'anonymisation service'.† The Information Commissioner, however, believes this option is feasible, a view supported by research conducted by the Scottish Executive Health Department.[13] In light of these findings, NHS Scotland is considering establishing this type of regime. It currently is proposing a system whereby all data required for national initiatives would be made anonymous by a central service, with local organisations having the option of either using the central service or establishing their own local anonymity service centres, which would apply nationally agreed standards of anonymity to data.

An additional option, for activities involving information held by secondary data repositories (such as disease registers), is for the information to be made anonymous by the relevant repository controller. Although this approach is obviously only suitable for projects using information available from these sources, a substantial amount of data is held in such repositories in the UK.‡ Again, however, this option raises privacy issues, as the data repositories would need to hold identifiable information.§ It also is

---

* To avoid breaching the Data Protection Act 1998, patients will need to consent to the service receiving their personal data, or the service will need to be exempted from the requirements of the Act under the Health and Social Care Act 2001, Section 60. There may be problems with relying on this legislation, however, if the government sticks to its promise that such exemptions would be few in number, time limited, and only given where there is no reasonable alternative (*see* Explanatory Notes to the Health and Social Care Act 2001).
** The capacity of intermediaries to respond to requests from data users for the reversal of pseudonyms was an area of particular concern for the Department of Health.[3]
† This was the opinion expressed in the majority of responses to the consultation paper on the anonymisation of patient information circulated by NHS Scotland.[13]
‡ The Department of Health has identified 250 separate registers of patient data, but estimates that the true number could be as high as 400.[3]
§ As with the specialised anonymity service, to avoid breaching the Data Protection Act 1998, patients will need to consent to the secondary data repositories receiving identifiable

dependent upon the different repository controllers having the capacity and skills to perform the work.

According to the Department of Health, the best approach in individual cases will differ depending upon the source and volume of information involved and the type of anonymity or pseudonymity required. For example, where the information is needed only for a healthcare provider's own internal purposes, such as internal service planning, and performance management and review, they can probably conduct the process themselves. An intermediary service, however, may be required for larger projects, especially those requiring the assignment of reversible pseudonyms to data obtained from multiple sources. Using an intermediary service in these circumstances not only avoids taxing healthcare providers' limited resources, but also removes the need to give individual healthcare providers access to the decoding key, which they would otherwise require to apply the pseudonyms consistently. Giving healthcare providers this key raises real privacy issues, as it enables them to re-identify any patient, not just those under the healthcare provider's own care. By contrast, using a single intermediary service ensures that reversals can be performed only at one secure location, a set-up much more likely to protect patients' privacy.

Advantages of anonymous information

Most secondary uses of patient information can be achieved using some form of anonymous or pseudonymous data.[3] Whilst it is often seen as a fallback option when patients' consent cannot be obtained, in many ways the use of anonymous or pseudonymous data can be a more effective way of safeguarding patient privacy. Although a consent-based privacy model sounds appealing, as it allows patients to determine the way their own information is used, it does not always work well in practice, as patients are frequently not well-placed to make these types of decisions.[17] Often, this is because they are not given sufficient information about the various activities to which they are expected to consent, or the security measures that will be in place.[18] Alternatively, having been given the necessary information, they may, for a number of reasons, have difficulty assessing what effects the disclosure will have on their privacy. For example, lack of knowledge about the health system's structure or operation may make it difficult for patients to understand what they are told. Equally, despite being worried or

information, or the data repositories will need to be exempted from the Act under the Health and Social Care Act 2001, Section 60.

confused, they may elect not to voice their concerns because of embarrassment or lack of confidence. Commonly, patients simply may fail to give the
matter proper consideration because of ill health, distress or other concerns
existing at the time consent is sought. This is particularly likely where
patients are expected to indicate their preference before or during their
consultation. By using anonymous information, however, none of these
problems arise, as the protection of privacy is based on the way the
information is presented, not on patients' ability or opportunity to make a
sound judgement.

The use of anonymous information also enables data users to avoid the
practical difficulties of securing consent. As discussed in Chapter 3, it can be
expensive and time-consuming to obtain informed, voluntary consent from
each patient for the wide variety of purposes for which medical records are
used. At the time patients' information is collected, healthcare providers are
often unaware of the specific ways their medical records will be used in
the future. Consent therefore will have to be obtained at some later stage,
which can be difficult, if not impossible, particularly where large numbers of
patients are involved, or a significant time has elapsed. This can not only
increase the cost of obtaining data for secondary activities, but also reduce
the quantity and quality of data available for these purposes.

A final advantage of using anonymous information is that it reduces the
risk that patient privacy will be compromised in the event of a security
breach.[19] Patients' willingness to have their medical information used for
secondary purposes is based on the assumption that the security of that
information will be strictly controlled, access being limited to authorised
personnel who have legitimate reasons for viewing it. However, despite
appropriate technical and policy arrangements, there is always the possibility that a system's security will be breached. This may result from an
outsider 'breaking into' the system, or, more commonly, misconduct or
carelessness on the part of authorised users. In either case, if identifiable
information is being used, such a breach could be very detrimental to the
patients involved (*see* Chapter 2, pp 23–4). Although unauthorised access to a
system containing anonymous information is still concerning, it is unlikely
to compromise patients' privacy, let alone cause them actual harm.

Patients' rights

The Data Protection Act 1998 grants patients the right to be informed of, and
object to, the way in which their personal data is used. Like all Data Protection
Act 1998 rights, this only applies to information that is capable of identifying
a patient. From a legal perspective, therefore, information that has been

made anonymous effectively can be used by healthcare providers without patients' knowledge or consent, and even in the face of explicit objections. There are some concerns, however, with the ethics of this approach.

Despite it being anonymous, patients may have valid reasons for wanting to prevent their information being used for certain purposes. Medical research, for example, may pursue causes that some patients find objectionable or offensive.[2] The study may be pursuing an aim that is inconsistent with a patient's religious or moral beliefs, such as improving contraceptive methods or investigating uses for blood.[12] Alternatively, patients may fear that the research could cause a certain group (of which they may be a member) to be stigmatised or treated prejudicially. Discoveries relating to the effects on health of specific genetic diseases could have this effect. Objections also can be based on less 'valid' grounds, which most people would not consider justify withholding important information. A disgruntled ex-employee, for example, may refuse to contribute in any way to particular research work purely because it is being conducted by the university or research institute from which they were dismissed. Equally, patients' privacy fears or distrust of government bodies may be such that the promise of anonymity is not enough to alleviate their concerns.

One way of dealing with this issue is to uphold only those objections that are based on valid grounds. However, there are many problems with this approach, the most fundamental being the difficulty of judging validity. For example, if one objection based on religious grounds is considered reasonable, should not all religious objections be treated the same way, irrespective of the nature of the belief or popularity of the particular faith?

In any event, it is doubtful whether patients should retain any control over their information once it has been made anonymous, irrespective of the source of their concerns. Patients do not own their medical information, they merely have certain rights over its use. These rights are derived from privacy considerations, which do not arise if the information is not capable of identifying the patient. In some respects, patients' position in relation to their anonymous medical information can be likened to that of taxpayers, who certainly do not have the right to object to the way in which their taxes are used. Once received into the pool of public funds, tax money ceases to be attributable to specific individuals and is used in the way the government sees fit. The fact that an individual taxpayer may object, often for very valid reasons, to certain government spending does not give them any right to control how their contribution is used, except through the power of the ballot box.

Most of the ethical guidelines relating to this issue recognise the importance of informing patients of how their information is used, but many are silent on the issue of patients' right to object. Of those that do address the issue, the General Medical Council and the British Medical Association do not appear to require that objections be respected, seeing consent and anonymity as separate alternatives for dealing with patient information.[7,16] Not surprisingly, patient advocacy groups adopt a very different stance, wanting all objections to the use of patient data to be upheld, even where that information is anonymous.*

The draft code of practice for NHS staff[20] does not deal with this point directly. It does, however, treat information very differently depending upon whether it is anonymous or identifiable. For example, patients' right to object to the way their medical information is used is recognised explicitly only in relation to the use or disclosure of 'confidential information that identifies them'.[20] Providing that patients' information has been made anonymous, therefore, the code appears to allow it to be used even though patients have not been so informed, and consent has not, or cannot, be obtained.

Box 10.2 outlines the spectrum of identifiability.

Box 10.2

Spectrum of identifiability

- Data containing uncoded identifiers, such as names and addresses.
- Data in which individuals are identified through a coded identifier, such as an NHS Number or local patient code. Although a patient's identity is not apparent on the face of the data, it can be obtained by accessing the reference list. The degree of protection this provides depends upon the availability of the reference list.
- Data in which individuals are identified through one-off encrypted pseudonyms, which are reversible with knowledge of the encryption rules. As above, the protection provided by this method depends upon the availability of the encryption rules.
- Data in which identifiers are replaced by pseudonyms that are produced through a one-way encryption facility, making it impossible to reverse the pseudonym and re-establish the patient's identity.
- Information from which all identifiers have been removed so that it is not possible to deduce the patient's identity or link information relating to the same individual.
- Aggregated data.

---

*For example, this was the view of the now abolished Association of Community Health Councils for England and Wales, which was established to represent the interests of patients in the health service (*see* ACHCEW's Position Statement on Patient Confidentiality, 2000).[11]

The way forward

Most sectors of the health industry recognise the benefits of making patient information anonymous, with the Department of Health,[3] the Information Commissioner[14] and various ethical and industry bodies[7,16,19] agreeing that, wherever possible, patients' data should be used in a non-identifiable form. According to the Department of Health, most health purposes that do not involve the direct care of patients can be achieved by using some type of anonymous or pseudonymous information.[3] Frequently, however, this does not occur.

One of the factors contributing to this situation is the continuing uncertainty as to whether de-identification merely provides an additional level of privacy protection, or whether it can be used as a valid alternative to obtaining consent. In theory, there is no reason why anonymity should not be an alternative to consent, provided it is carried out effectively and consistently. For it to become a viable option, upon which healthcare providers can rely confidently, further guidance is required as to what degree of anonymity is considered both legally and ethically acceptable, and the optimum way of achieving this standard. It is hoped that the Department of Health's 'pseudonymisation toolkit' will clarify some of this uncertainty.

Summary:

- Most secondary purposes for which patient information is required can be achieved by using some form of anonymous or pseudonymous data.
- Information is anonymous if there are no reasonable possibility that it can be linked to the patient to whom it relates. There is some uncertainty as to what is required to meet this standard and what will be considered a reasonable possibility of identification.
- Pseudonymous data are data in which the patient's identity is replaced with an arbitrary code, which identifies the patient in the system, but from which they cannot readily be identified in the real world.
- Anonymous data are not subject to the restrictions of the Data Protection Act 1998 or the duty of confidentiality. The legal status of pseudonymous data is yet to be determined in the UK.

- Making data anonymous can involve considerable time and expertise. For large projects, it may be best for this work to be performed by a specialist service.
- In many ways, making data anonymous protects patients' privacy more effectively than obtaining patient consent.
- There is some disagreement as to whether patients should have any control over the use that can be made of their anonymous data.

References

1 The Caldicott Committee (1997) *Report on the Review of Patient-identifiable Information.* NHS Executive. (www.doh.gov.uk/confiden/crep.html). (Accessed 5 August 2003.)

2 Lowrance W (2002) *Learning from Experience – privacy and the secondary use of data in health research.* The Nuffield Trust, London.

3 Information Policy Unit (2002) *Options for the Pseudonymisation of Patient Identifiable Information (Draft) Version 1.1.* Department of Health, London.

4 Goldman J and Choy A (2002) *Privacy and Confidentiality in Health Research.* The Online Ethics Center for Engineering and Science, Case Western Reserve University. (http://onlineethics.org/reseth/nbac/hgoldman.html#f3). (Accessed 30 May 2003.)

5 NHS Information Authority (2002) *Caring for Information – model for the future.* (www.nhsia.nhs.uk/confidentiality/pages/consultation/docs/caring_model.pdf). (Accessed 8 July 2003.)

6 Information Commissioner (2002) *Use and Disclosure of Health Data.* (www.dataprotection.gov.uk/dpr/dpdoc.nsf), under 'Compliance Advice'. (Accessed 10 May 2003.)

7 General Medical Council (2000) *Confidentiality: protecting and providing information.* GMC, London.

8 Department of Health (DoH) (2001) *Building the Information Core: protecting and using confidential information – a strategy for the NHS.* (www.doh.gov.uk/ipu/confiden/strategyv7.pdf). (Accessed 10 June 2003.)

9 Davies S (2001) *Taking Liberties in Confidence, a Report for the Nuffield Trust on the Implications of Clause 67 of the Health and Social Care Bill.* (http://is.lse.ac.uk/privacy/healthconfidentiality.doc). (Accessed 23 June 2003.)

10 Information Policy Unit (2003) *Draft NHS Number Policy Statement Vol.5, HRDG 025/2003.* Department of Health, London. (www.doh.gov.uk/ipu/ahr/hrdg2503.pdf). (Accessed 21 July 2003.)

11 Cambridge Health Informatics Limited (2001) *Gaining Patient Consent to Disclosure.* (www.doh.gov.uk/ipu/confiden/gpcd/exec/gpcdexec.pdf). (Accessed 13 March 2003.)

12 Chester M (2000) Patients' expectations and experiences (ACHCEW contribution). In: *Privacy in the Electronic NHS.* (Debate organised by the British Medical Informatics Society, London, 30 November 2000.) (www.bmis.org/privacy 2000/chester.doc). (Accessed 10 April 2003.)

13 Confidentiality and Security Advisory Group for Scotland (2002) *Protecting Patient Confidentiality – final report.* Scottish Executive Health Department. (www.show.scot.nhs.uk/sehd/publications/ppcr/ppcr.pdf). (Accessed 6 August 2003.)

14 Information Commissioner (1998) *Data Protection Act 1998: legal guidance.* Version 1. (www.dataprotection.gov.uk/dpr/dpdoc.nsf), under 'Legal Guidance'. (Accessed 30 March 2003.)

15 Information Policy Unit (undated) *Pseudonymisation of Patient Level Data – a toolkit for requestors and providers of data.* Department of Health, London.

16 British Medical Association (1999) *Confidentiality and Disclosure of Health Information.* BMA, London.

17 Starr P (1999) Privacy and access to information: striking the right balance in healthcare. In: *Massachusetts Health Data Consortium, 4th Annual Meeting,* Boston, MA, 16 April. (www.nchica.org/HIPAAResources/Samples/privacylessons/ P-101%20Massachusetts%20Health%20Data%20Consortium.htm). (Accessed 13 September 2003.)

18 Institute of Medicine (1994) *Health Data in the Information Age.* National Academy Press, Washington DC.

19 Medical Research Council (2000) *Personal Information in Medical Research.* (Updated January 2003.) (www.mrc.ac.uk/pdf-pimr.pdf).

20 Department of Health (DoH) (2002) *Confidentiality: a code of practice for NHS staff (draft).* (www.nhsia.nhs.uk/confidentiality/pages/consultation/docs/code_ prac.pdf). (Accessed 24 June 2003.)

Chapter 11

Freedom of information

At the same time as access to personal information is becoming more restricted, access to government information is expanding. The Freedom of Information Act 2000, which will come into full effect in 2005, will open the way for all members of the public to access information held by government bodies, including the NHS.

For the most part, this will be very beneficial. NHS organisations produce and use a great deal of information that could be of interest to the public. Having access to information relating to financial and management decisions, for example, may help the public to understand the challenges facing the health service and to assess the standard of care being provided. At the same time, however, the NHS also holds vast amounts of confidential patient data, both in actual medical records and within confidential reports and studies, which should not be open to the public. Although this type of information is exempt from the Freedom of Information Act 2000, this legislation could compromise patient privacy if requests for information are not handled carefully.

Freedom of Information Act 2000

For many years, the UK government has operated within a culture of secrecy.[1] To some degree, this is acceptable, as a certain level of privacy is needed to protect the interests of the country. Increasingly, however, it is recognised that unnecessary secrecy leads to arrogant governance and defective decision-making. It also erodes public confidence in the government's ability, integrity and effectiveness, and conflicts with the growing expectation within the community of a transparent government that is accountable to the public it seeks to represent.

The Freedom of Information Act 2000 aims to increase the openness and transparency of government departments and bodies (called 'public authorities')* by making the information they hold publicly available. This

*Freedom of Information Act 2000, Section 3.

is achieved in two ways. First, all public authorities must produce a publication scheme, which is a list of classes of information it routinely makes available to the public, with details of how to obtain that information and any applicable charges.* In the health sector, such schemes were to be published by October 2003. Second, from January 2005, public authorities must make all information they hold, except that which is classified as exempt, available on request.** Requests can be made by any member of the public, regardless of their interest in the information or the purpose for which they seek access to it.

Although freedom of information legislation is relatively new in the UK, the idea of making some government information available to the public is not. Since 1994, many government bodies, including the Department of Health, have operated under a non-statutory freedom of information regime, known as the Code of Practice on Access to Government Information.[2] The new legislation, however, establishes a more integral and straightforward method of obtaining this data.

In the health sector, an important difference between the Freedom of Information Act 2000 and the Code is the Act's more extensive application, covering all NHS bodies, from hospitals and general practice surgeries, to dentists, pharmacists and opticians.[†] This means that there is a single set of rules applying to the Department of Health, each individual NHS organisation and all other public authorities, making it easier for members of the public to understand, and therefore use, their right to access government information. As the Act is overseen by the Information Commissioner, it also provides a more direct and accessible mechanism for enforcing access rights.[‡]

These and other changes introduced by the Act should improve the openness and accountability of government bodies substantially. For the Act to be effective, all public authorities, including the NHS, must ensure they have made the preparations needed to enable them to meet their new obligations.

---

* Freedom of Information Act 2000, Section 19.
** Freedom of Information Act 2000, Section 1.
† *See* the definition of 'public authority' in Freedom of Information Act 2000, Section 3.
‡ Under the Code, complaints could be made to the Parliamentary Ombudsman, though this had to be done through a Member of Parliament. The Freedom of Information Act 2000, however, allows aggrieved individuals to approach the Information Commissioner directly (*see* Freedom of Information Act 2000, Parts IV and V).

Freedom of information and the National Health Service

The NHS is a particularly important branch of the public service. The lives of most people are affected, both directly and indirectly, by the efficiency and effectiveness of NHS organisations, the decisions they make, and the way in which their limited resources are used. Thus there is likely to be quite a high level of interest in accessing NHS data, with requests for information expected from individual patients, patient advocate groups and journalists. The Freedom of Information Act 2000 may also open up access to information about health and drug risks that are reported by hospitals or presented to the Department of Health or other government bodies.* In other countries, freedom of information legislation has been used as a means of accessing one's own medical record,[5] although in the UK such requests will continue to be governed by the Data Protection Act 1998.**

The Lord Chancellor's Advisory Group on the implementation of the Freedom of Information Act 2000 is confident that the NHS will be able to adapt to the new regime.[6] According to this Group, NHS bodies are 'well placed'[6] to meet the freedom of information requirements, having responded to similar requests for data under information-sharing codes. Although the Group acknowledges that the Act will require some changes to be made to the way in which patient records are managed, it is confident that recent initiatives designed to improve record management procedures will ensure that the NHS is prepared for this.

To some degree, this optimism is well placed. In many respects the freedom of information obligations will simply be an escalation of the more open and accountable way of operating that is already being encouraged within the NHS. As the Lord Chancellor's Advisory Group noted, NHS organisations have been complying with information-sharing obligations since 1995 under the Code of Practice on Openness in the NHS,[7] which complements the access code to which the Department of Health is subject. In 1997, the Caldicott Committee recommended that the NHS be more open about the way it uses patient data,[8] a recommendation now largely reflected in the requirements of the Data Protection Act 1998. It also has been mandatory, since 1998, for NHS trust meetings to be conducted in public.[†]

---

* There are many groups pushing for this information to be made more publicly available.[3,4]
** Information is exempt if it relates to personal data of which the applicant is the data subject (Freedom of Information Act 2000, Section 40(1)).
[†] Public Bodies (Admission to Meetings) (NHS Trusts) Order 1997, which adds NHS trusts to the list of bodies covered by the Public Bodies (Admission to Meetings) Act 1960.

The freedom of information regime of information-sharing does, however, impose some new obligations on the NHS. The most significant challenge it is likely to face is the need to balance the obligation to disclose information with the duty to protect the confidentiality of patient data. Although these obligations need not necessarily conflict (as the Freedom of Information Act 2000 respects the privacy of personal data), responding to freedom of information requests will not always be a straightforward task. Mistakes will be made, to the detriment of patient privacy, if each NHS organisation is not fully aware of its own obligations and properly equipped to manage them. Whilst the Lord Chancellor's Advisory Group may be confident that the NHS can meet this challenge, its optimism may be somewhat misplaced, given the difficulties the NHS has encountered in trying to comply with its obligations under the Data Protection Act 1998.

Freedom of information and patient records

As a general rule, the new Acts cannot be used to access patients' medical records, as most information contained in such records is exempt from disclosure. This will not prevent patients accessing their own records under the Data Protection Act 1998, but it will ensure that, in most cases, attempts by third parties to obtain patient data will be refused. Refusal will usually be based on the fact that providing access to the information would infringe the data protection principles* or breach an obligation of confidentiality.** In some cases, information may be withheld on the basis that releasing it is prohibited by other legislation,[†] such as the Adoption Act 1976, the Abortion Act 1967 or the Anatomy Act 1984. Given these explicit exemptions, direct requests for clearly personal documents, such as medical records and test results, will rarely be successful and therefore pose little threat to patient privacy.

Of much more concern is the possibility that identifiable patient data could be released in response to requests for other types of information held by the NHS. Research findings, hospital performance tables, and information considered in internal enquiries or policy decisions could all contain information that either directly or indirectly identifies individual patients. Although such information is exempt from the Freedom of Information Act 2000 disclosure requirements, in the same way as if it were part of a medical

---

*Freedom of Information Act 2000, Section 40.
**Freedom of Information Act 2000, Section 41.
[†] Freedom of Information Act 2000, Section 44.

record, being contained in non-medical documents may increase the risk that it could be overlooked and accidentally released.

The problem of identifying the boundary between public and private information, and the associated risk of releasing private patient data, was raised by the British Medical Association (BMA) in its response to the government's freedom of information White Paper.[9] The BMA was concerned that the government had not drawn sufficient attention to the seriousness of releasing confidential or personal data to third parties. Although such information must sometimes be released for public interest reasons, the circumstances in which this occurs should be strictly controlled, in accordance with current guidelines. Similar sentiments were expressed by the NHS Confederation, a body representing the majority of managers in NHS trusts and health authorities, which stressed the importance of ensuring that the legislation not be allowed to 'undermine the giving of information in confidence, which is at the heart of much of the information (usually personal) used within the NHS'.[10]

The Information Commissioner also has acknowledged the potential difficulties of dealing with patient data and other personal information under the Freedom of Information Act 2000, urging public authorities to 'exercise caution'[11] in this area. The Commissioner recognises that some access requests will give rise to 'a tension between the rights of an individual under the DPA and the duties of a public authority to disclose information under the Act'.[11]

At the same time, however, the Act might also allow campaigners to obtain information that helps improve the way patient information is protected. The ability to access information about NHS decision-making, consultations and reports can enable privacy campaigners to uncover information that can be used to push for improved privacy protection. Recently, for example, the Campaign for Freedom of Information was able to obtain reports prepared for ministers about the fees charged to patients for accessing their own medical records under the Data Protection Act 1998.[12] Although this request was made under the Code rather than the Freedom of Information Act 2000, the initial refusal of the Department of Health to supply the information (supposedly on the basis of the privacy of internal discussions) demonstrates the importance of having a clear, statutory right of access with effective enforcement and appeals procedures, as is provided by the new legislation.

Anonymous data

As the exemptions in the Freedom of Information Act 2000 apply to information not documents, the presence of exempt information should not prevent an entire document being released, just certain portions of it.[11] Wherever possible, exempt information should be masked or removed from a document, thus enabling the remainder of it to be provided to the applicant. Potentially, this principle could require that healthcare providers disclose documents containing patient data where it is possible to remove the identifying variables. As full anonymity can be difficult to achieve, this could have a significant effect on patient privacy.

In Chapter 10, making data anonymous was advanced as an effective method of protecting patient privacy when using data for research, disease monitoring, and other legitimate health sector initiatives. The slight risk of identification, which often remains despite this process, is acceptable, given the importance of these activities and the fact that they are conducted in a regulated and supervised manner. Disclosing anonymous data in response to a freedom of information application, however, raises very different considerations.

Information can be accessed under the Freedom of Information Act 2000 by any person, for any purpose. Applicants need not give an explanation as to why they require the information, or what they intend to do with it,[13] and upon receiving it can use it in any way they wish, subject only to the general constraints of defamation and similar laws. Disclosing information in response to a freedom of information application, therefore, even one made by a single, private individual, potentially releases that information into the public domain. Consequently, a slight risk that a patient could be identified from anonymous information takes on a very different meaning. As a result, the BMA has cautioned against releasing anonymous, or even aggregated, data under the Act, seeing anonymity as an appropriate method of protecting patient privacy only in the case of medical research.[9]

The risks associated with releasing anonymous data in response to a freedom of information request are further increased by the fact that there are few limits on the number of freedom of information applications that can be made by a single individual or organisation.* It is therefore possible for one individual to accrue separate items of information, through multiple applications, that together identify a patient. It would be extremely difficult for a healthcare provider to assess the risk of this occurring, particularly where the applications are made over a period of time.

An additional problem with disclosing anonymous information under the Act is that third parties, such as patients, who may be affected by the disclosure, have no right to be informed of the application's existence or

---

* A single individual or organisation can make multiple freedom of information applications to the same public authority, provided the applications are not identical or substantially similar (Freedom of Information Act 2000, Section 14).

the decision to release the requested data. The 'best practice' guidelines for dealing with freedom of information applications, developed by the Lord Chancellor's Department,[14] advise public authorities to consult affected third parties when confidential information is requested or where the views of the third party may be relevant, but it is questionable whether this would (or could) be followed in the case of anonymous data. By having decided to disclose the information, the healthcare provider obviously is satisfied that the patient's identity is concealed sufficiently, thus making it unnecessary, in the public authority's judgement, to consider the patient's opinion. It may also be impractical to consult with patients if the document in question contains anonymous data from several individuals. In any event, even if a patient is consulted, he or she has no right of appeal should the public authority decide to release the information.

From a patient privacy perspective, therefore, anonymous personal data should, ideally, be exempt from the Freedom of Information Act 2000. If not, it should at least be necessary to make anonymous any information derived from patients to a very high level before it is disclosed for freedom of information purposes. As this issue has not been legally considered, however, it is difficult for healthcare providers to determine the correct course of action.

Dealing with a freedom of information application

Figure 11.1 (overleaf) summarises the main decisions that need to be made when processing a freedom of information application. The issues are presented in a simplified form to provide a general overview of the topic. The flowchart is not intended to provide a full summary of the Freedom of Information Act 2000 or a comprehensive guide for dealing with applications made under it.

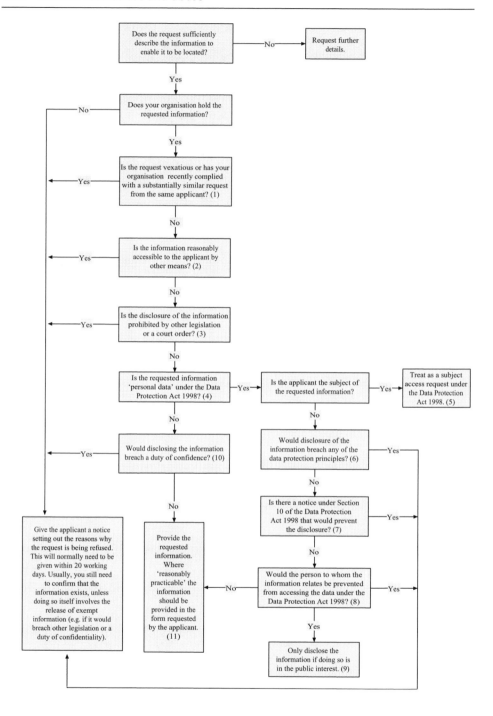

Figure 11.1 (opposite): Dealing with a freedom of information application. Key: 1 = An application may be vexatious if it is made with a malicious intent or for the sole purpose of annoying the public authority. It is not vexatious merely because it is difficult to see why the applicant would want the requested information, considerable effort is required to retrieve the information, or it could cause the public authority some embarrassment. 2 = Whether information is reasonably accessed by other means is affected by the applicant's circumstances. The availability of the information on the internet or by inspection at a particular office will not be sufficient in all cases. Information may be considered reasonably accessible even though payment is required. 3 = For example, legislation prevents the disclosure of certain information relating to adoptions, assisted reproductive practices and investigations by the Health Service Ombudsman. The disclosure of information may also be prohibited by court injunction. 4 = Put simply, does it relate to an identifiable living individual? For the full definition of personal data, *see* the Data Protection Act 1998, Section 1(1). 5 = This means that the exceptions and procedures set out in the Data Protection Act 1998 apply to the application, rather than those in the Freedom of Information Act 2000. It does not mean that the applicant has to submit a new application referring to the Data Protection Act 1998. 6 = For example, would the disclosure be considered unfair processing (in breach of the first data protection principle), or a further processing of the information that is incompatible with the purpose for which it was collected (in breach of the second data protection principle)? 7 = This is a notice from a data subject requiring a data controller to stop the processing of certain personal data on the basis that the processing is likely to cause that person or another person substantial, unwarranted damage or distress. 8 = For example, because it will cause serious harm to the physical or mental health of the patient or another person. 9 = Does the public interest in not communicating the information outweigh the public interest in communicating it? Factors that may support disclosing the information include the potential for this to further understanding of a current public issue, to facilitate the accountability of government decision-making or public spending, or uncover information affecting public safety. Factors discouraging disclosure may include the information being incomplete and therefore likely to mislead, or the negative effect the disclosure will have on the authority's ability to function. 10 = This duty prevents confidential information that was disclosed in circumstances of confidence from being used for any purpose other than that for which is was disclosed, without the confider's permission. This could include information imparted by patients to their doctors, documents disclosed under confidentiality agreements or information relating to confidential commercial discussions. 11 = What is reasonably practicable depends on all the circumstances, including cost. Where it is not considered reasonably practicable, reasons must be given to the applicant and the information must then be communicated by any means that are reasonable in the circumstances, having regard to the nature of the information and the circumstances of both the public authority and the applicant.

Summary

- All NHS organisations will have to make certain information available to the public under the Freedom of Information Act 2000.
- Patient data will usually be classified as exempt and should not be disclosed.
- NHS organisations must be careful when balancing their freedom of information obligation to disclose information and their confidentiality and Data Protection Act 1998 obligations.
- Releasing anonymous data under the Freedom of Information Act 2000 may be detrimental to patients' privacy.

References

1 UK Government White Paper (1997) *Your Right to Know: the Government's proposals for a Freedom of Information Act.* (www.archive.official-documents.co.uk/document/caboff/foi/foi.htm). (Accessed 11 September 2003.)

2 Department for Constitutional Affairs (1997) *Open Government: the code of practice on access to government information.* (www.lcd.gov.uk/foi/ogcode981.htm). (Accessed 11 September 2003.)

3 Abraham J, Sheppard J and Reed T (1999) Rethinking transparency and accountability in medicines regulation in the United Kingdom. *British Medical Journal.* **318**: 46.

4 McKee M (1999) Secret government revisited. *British Medical Journal.* **318**: 1712.

5 Lord Chancellor's Department (1997) *Your Right to Know: background material.* (www.lcd.gov.uk/foi/bg_cont.htm). (Accessed 11 September 2003.)

6 Lord Chancellor's Advisory Group on Implementation of the Freedom of Information Act (2002) *Annual Report on Bringing Fully into Force those Provisions of the FOIA 2000 which are Not Yet Fully in Force.* (www.lcd.gov.uk/foi/impgroup/foiag02-17.pdf). (Accessed 9 September 2003.)

7 NHS Executive (1999) *Code of Practice on Openness in the NHS.* (www.doh.gov.uk/nhsexec/codemain.htm). (Accessed 15 September 2003.)

8 The Caldicott Committee (1997) *Report on the Review of Patient-identifiable Information.* NHS Executive. (www.doh.gov.uk/confiden/crep.html). (Accessed 5 August 2003.)

9 Lowe M, British Medical Association (1998) Letter to R Cayzer, Freedom of Information Unit, 27 February. On: 'Have Your Say' website: responses to the government's FOI consultation paper. (http://foi.democracy.org.uk/html/submission303.html). (Accessed 15 September 2003.)

10 Derek D, NHS Confederation (1998) Letter to D Clark, Chancellor of the Duchy of Lancaster, 26 February. On: 'Have Your Say' website: responses to the government's FOI consultation paper. (http://foi.democracy.org.uk/html/submission342.html). (Accessed 15 September 2003.)

11 Information Commissioner (2003) *The Freedom of Information Act 2000: an introduction*. Office of the Information Commissioner, Cheshire.

12 Campaign for Freedom of Information (2003) *Broken Commitments on Access to Health Records*. (www.cfoi.org.uk/dohltr100103.html). (Accessed 15 September 2003.)

13 Information Commissioner (2001) *Freedom of Information Act 2000: media brief*. Office of the Information Commissioner, Cheshire.

14 Lord Chancellor's Department (2002) *Code of Practice on the Discharge of Public Authorities' Functions under Part 1 of the Freedom of Information Act 2000 – dealing with requests for information*. (www.lcd.gov.uk/foi/codesprac.htm). (Accessed 16 September 2003.)

Chapter 12

The best way forward

The protection of patient confidentiality is the cornerstone of effective healthcare, though this must be balanced with the need to use information in other contexts. Many groups have legitimate reasons for seeking access to patient data, including healthcare providers, administrators, researchers, law enforcement agencies, auditors and policy makers, and their work often benefits the whole community, including, indirectly, patients themselves. Individual patients, however, have equally legitimate rights to limit the extent to which their personal and sensitive medical data are used. Resolving this apparent conflict poses the greatest challenge to all those involved in patient care; a problem made all the more difficult by the complexity of the healthcare environment, and the constantly changing legal, social and ethical framework that applies, not only to the future use of medical records, but frequently to large numbers of retrospective records as well.

In juggling these issues it is useful to consider three key principles.

Transparency

Patients must be informed, and kept informed, of the way in which their medical data are used and by whom. Unnecessary secrecy, whether intentional or not, will lead to distrustful, cynical patients and complacent, irresponsible data users. An open, transparent system, on the other hand, should promote trust, engender a greater sense of patient involvement and lead to more responsible practices. Ultimately this should improve the quality of care that can be provided and patients' healthcare experiences.

Establishing such a system is not easy, and it requires that all patients be informed fully of the way their information is used and that their consent be obtained. This is a major undertaking requiring a substantial investment of time and money (*see* Chapter 3, pp 38–9). It should be treated as a national issue, not left to individual, local organisations. The arguments are complex and there is a danger that even a well-delivered message could be hijacked by a small, yet vociferous minority lobby who are prepared to resort to the scare tactics of the 'information terrorist'.

We would envisage that a national information campaign would provide the start for discussion of the issues. This approach would minimise local costs, deliver a consistent message and avoid unnecessary duplication of work. In some instances, local initiatives may mean that specific areas are best implemented by individual trusts,[1] which provides the added advantage of improving patients' understanding of the way their own local organisation manages their data.

As discussed in Chapter 3, the large number and diversity of NHS patients means that this information will need to be disseminated through a range of different communication methods, each with a different level of detail.* This approach should ensure that all patients, even those who have not used an NHS service for some time, receive at least a minimum level of information about the way their health information is used. Although running the information campaign will involve significant expense, this will decline after the initial phase, as the bulk of the campaign materials will have been prepared and the level of publicity can be scaled down.

On its own, however, a transparent system is not enough to protect patients' privacy. There is little benefit in being open about the way patient information is managed, if there is no way to stop it being used inappropriately or in ways that threaten patients' dignity and autonomy. To ensure this does not occur, transparency must be supported by consent and anonymity.

Anonymous information

Many analyses can be performed on anonymous data and therefore, wherever possible, patient data should be used in this form. Before data is released, either for an organisation's own internal purposes or for some external project or activity, an assessment should be made of whether anonymous or pseudonymous data could be used. When de-identifying records, as many personal identifiers as possible should be removed, those remaining being included out of necessity not convenience.**

Data that has been made anonymous to an acceptable level can be used without patient consent. However, in the interests of maintaining a transparent system, patients still should be informed of the way their anonymous

---

* This type of communication strategy was recommended by studies commissioned by the Scottish NHS [1] and the NHS Executive.[2]

** This view is shared by the Department of Health,[3] the Information Commissioner[4] and various ethical and industry groups (see, for example, the General Medical Council,[5] the Medical Research Council[6] and the British Medical Association).[7]

information will be used, as well as the standards and safeguards that will be employed to protect their identity. It is essential to be aware of the possibility that a patient may become identifiable if anonymous data from two sources are merged or if an analysis reveals a case with unique clinical features or social circumstances that is applicable to just one individual.

To work effectively, healthcare providers need a way of reliably determining whether an acceptable level of anonymity has been reached. One way would be to follow the approach used in the USA where legislation sets out the specific criteria that must be satisfied for data to be classified as anonymous.* Data are deemed to be acceptably anonymous if either a qualified statistician has certified this to be the case, or the identifiers listed in the Act have been removed.**

The use of pseudonymous data is another option, but it is essential that the key to unlocking patients' identities be kept securely and separately from the substantive information. Making data pseudonymous can be complex, which makes it more difficult to identify possible risks to privacy, and increases the need for special privacy safeguards. For this reason, the Department of Health has suggested that all major pseudonymisation work be performed by a central service established for this purpose.[3]

Even where records have been made acceptably anonymous, this ought not to entitle data users to deal with them in any way they like, as there is usually some risk that patients could still be identified.[1] In the case of specific, health-related research, disease monitoring, auditing and similar activities, this risk of identification is usually considered acceptable, as the activities are of particular benefit to the community and involve the disclosure of data to only a limited number of people. The situation is very different where information is to be made available to the general public. Disclosure requirements for these purposes need a higher standard of anonymity, such as aggregation or the suppression of data containing small numbers of cases.

As an additional safeguard, anonymous information should only ever be disclosed to external organisations under an agreement that sets out the specific purpose for which it is required, and the security measures that will be employed to protect it from misuse.[†] The organisation

---

* Privacy Rule, 45 CFR Section 164.514 (2002). For further details, *see* Chapter 10, p. 138.
** Included in the list are the patient's (or a relative's, employer's or household member's) name, phone or fax number, email address, social security or medical record number, and 'any other unique identifying number, characteristic or code' (Privacy Rule, 45 CFR Section 164.514(b) (2002)).
† In the USA, de-identified data can be disclosed only under an agreement in which recipients, among other things, specify their intended uses and disclosures, name who will be using the data, commit to certain safeguards, and agree not to attempt to identify or contact the patients (Privacy Rule, 45 CFR Section 164.514(e) (2002)).

should be entitled to use the information only in accordance with that agreement.

In circumstances where anonymous or pseudonymous information cannot be used, due, for example, to the nature of the activity being conducted or the characteristics of the particular data set,* the patient's consent (and, in some cases, the approval of a local or national ethics committee) will be required.

Consent

The gold standard for the use of identifiable medical information is a consent-based model, which gives patients full control over the extent to which the privacy of their own data is protected. This maintains the patient's sense of autonomy and involvement in their healthcare, and allows individual differences and concerns to be accommodated.[8] However, as discussed in Chapter 3, obtaining express consent for all uses of patient information is difficult and expensive.** To minimise these problems, the authors propose a tiered system that prescribes different forms of consent for different types of activities.

In the uppermost tier lie those activities that are essential to treating patients or to the continued ability of the healthcare system to deliver medical care. Given the importance of these activities, it is acceptable for treatment to be made conditional upon consent being given. Patients must understand that if they wish to withhold their consent, the standard of their treatment cannot be guaranteed.[†] Although this consent can be implied from patients' willingness to receive treatment (provided, of course, that they have been informed of these activities), it may be preferable for them to sign an acknowledgement form indicating that they have read and understood the information provided. The activities and disclosures in this acknowledgement should be clearly distinguished from any truly optional uses of information for which patients' specific consent would be sought. At the moment the NHS fails to differentiate clearly between voluntary uses of information and those that are core to the delivery of effective care. This confusion casts doubt on the whole value of consent forms (*see* Chapter 3, pp 45–6).

---

* It may, for example, be difficult to achieve an acceptable level of anonymity where the particular data items or combination of data items are very unusual.
** The total cost has been estimated at £400 million.[2]
† This view is shared by the Information Commissioner.[9]

In the second tier of our consent model are the bulk of activities not directly related to the provision of medical treatment to an individual, such as research, training and health monitoring. Patients should be given a real choice as to whether they will allow their data to be used in these ways. To enable patients to make a meaningful decision, the activities need to be described quite specifically, though it is unnecessary, and often impossible, to set out every detail. With research, for example, it would be sufficient to inform patients of the types of bodies that usually conduct medical research, the purposes for which this research is carried out, and the minimum privacy and security restrictions that will be employed to protect their data. It is not necessary to list the precise conditions or treatments being investigated, or the specific bodies that will conduct the work, as often this will not be known at the time consent is sought, and will make the consent unnecessarily restrictive. However, because these details could be important to some patients, patients should be allowed to limit the scope or duration of their consent. Medical record systems must therefore be designed to deal with individual preferences, and where they cannot, as will often be the case with paper files, patients' conditional consent ought to be treated as a refusal.

The final tier covers a limited number of activities that, by law, do not require patient consent to use identifiable data. These include mandatory disclosures to health monitoring bodies, disclosures for judicial proceedings or law enforcement purposes, and disclosures justified by the public interest. Whilst the government will always have the power to include additional activities in this list, through the enactment of new legislation, this should be done only as a matter of necessity, not convenience. General powers to override the need for consent, such as that established by the Health and Social Care Act 2001, are controversial and almost certainly will prove transitory as better consent systems and anonymity processes are introduced. At present these non-specific powers may have created more problems than they solve, although the role of specific monitoring bodies, such as the Patient Information Advisory Group (PIAG) and the Security and Confidentiality Advisory Group (SCAG), is to be welcomed.

Are we on track?

Significant progress has been made throughout the NHS, although obviously there is still a long way to go before it truly can be said to provide a comprehensive privacy environment. The preceding chapters refer to a number of policy documents and strategies being developed by the Department of Health and various NHS organisations and committees that aim to improve the way patient information is used in the health sector.[10,11,12,13,14]

Despite leaving a number of questions unanswered, these documents suggest ways that have the potential to bring about significant improvements. Whether or not they do will largely depend upon how effectively they are implemented and enforced. A strategy is of little benefit, regardless of how impressive and ambitious it may be on paper, if it is not put into practice properly. The ultimate success of the government's plans, therefore, will depend greatly upon what occurs over the coming years.

The issues are inevitably complex and there is still a long way to go, but considerable reassurance should be derived from the fact that the management and protection of patient data has become a priority issue for the NHS. This in itself is an important step toward establishing a health system that protects patient privacy, and this book is one component of these advances.

References

1 Confidentiality and Security Advisory Group for Scotland (2002) *Protecting Patient Confidentiality – final report.* Scottish Executive Health Department. (www.show.scot.nhs.uk/sehd/publications/ppcr/ppcr.pdf). (Accessed 6 August 2003.)

2 Cambridge Health Informatics Limited (2001) *Gaining Patient Consent to Disclosure.* (www.doh.gov.uk/ipu/confiden/gpcd/exec/gpcdexec.pdf). (Accessed 13 March 2003.)

3 Information Policy Unit (2002) *Options for the Pseudonymisation of Patient Identifiable Information (Draft) Version 1.1.* Department of Health, London.

4 Information Commissioner (1998) *Data Protection Act 1998: legal guidance.* Version 1. (www.dataprotection.gov.uk/dpr/dpdoc.nsf), under 'Legal Guidance'. (Accessed 30 March 2003.)

5 General Medical Council (2000) *Confidentiality: protecting and providing information.* GMC, London.

6 Medical Research Council (2000) *Personal Information in Medical Research.* (Updated January 2003.) (www.mrc.ac.uk/pdf-pimr.pdf).

7 British Medical Association (1999) *Confidentiality and Disclosure of Health Information.* BMA, London.

8 NHS Information Authority, The Consumers' Association, Health Which? (2002) *Share with Care – people's views on consent and confidentiality of patient information.* (www.nhsia.nhs.uk/confidentiality/pages/docs/swc.pdf). (Accessed 20 August 2003.)

9 Information Commissioner (2002) *Use and Disclosure of Health Data.* (www.dataprotection.gov.uk/dpr/dpdoc.nsf), under 'Compliance Advice'. (Accessed 10 May 2003.)

10 NHS Information Authority (1998) *Information for Health.* (www.nhsia.nhs.uk/ def/pages/info4health/contents/asp). (Accessed 10 June 2003.)

11 Department of Health (DoH) (2001) *Building the Information Core: protecting and using confidential patient information – a strategy for the NHS.* (www.doh.gov.uk/ ipu/confiden/strategyv7.pdf). (Accessed 10 June 2003.)

12 Department of Health (DoH) (2002) *Confidentiality: a code of practice for NHS staff (draft).* (www.nhsia.nhs.uk/confidentiality/pages/consultation/docs/code_ prac.pdf). (Accessed 24 June 2003.)

13 NHS Information Authority (2002) *Caring for Information – model for the future.* (www.nhsia.nhs.uk/confidentiality/pages/consultation/docs/caring_ model.pdf). (Accessed 8 July 2003.)

14 Department of Health (DoH) (2001) *Building the Information Core – implementing the NHS plan.* (www.nhsia.nhs.uk/pdf/info-core.pdf). (Accessed 10 June 2003.)

Index